The Complete Boating Guide to the Connecticut River

Second Edition

Edited by
Mark C. Borton
Brian E. Becker
Tim Scannell
Gene Mitchell

The Connecticut River
Watershed Council

Embassy Marine Publishing

The Complete Boating Guide to the Connecticut River, 2nd Edition

Copyright © 1990
The Connecticut River Watershed Council, Inc.
and Embassy Imprint, Inc.

Edited by Mark C. Borton, Brian E. Becker,
    Tim Scannell, Gene Mitchell

Book Design by Susan Smith

Cover Design by Nancy Close

Cover Illustration and Maps by Robert Sorenson

Production Manager Nancy Close

Library of Congress Card Catalog No. 86-070240
ISBN 0-9616371-1-0
Printed in The United States of America
First Printing May 1986
Second Printing July 1990

Connecticut River Watershed Council, Inc.
125 Combs Road
Easthampton, MA 01027
(413) 584-0057

Embassy Marine Publishing
P.O. Box 338
Essex, CT 06426
(203) 395-0188

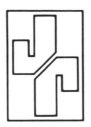

JAMES RIVER CORPORATION

Printing Papers suitable for a wide variety of end-use applications:

Commercial Printing
Quick Print
In Plant
Office Copying

Call your local paper merchant for these printing papers:

Richmond Bond/Offset
Richmond Opaque
Richmond Index, Tag, Vellum Bristol
Word Pro Xerographic Papers

The Connecticut River Watershed Council wishes to acknowledge with gratitude the generous contributions of the following institutions. Without their donations *The Complete Boating Guide to the Connecticut River* would not have been possible.

Asea Brown Boveri (formerly Combustion Engineering)

Hallmark Cards, Inc.

Heublein Foundation, Inc.

James River Corporation

New England Power Company

North Central Connecticut Tobacco Valley Convention and Visitors Center

Northeast Utilities

Stanley Works

The State of Connecticut, Department of Environmental Protection

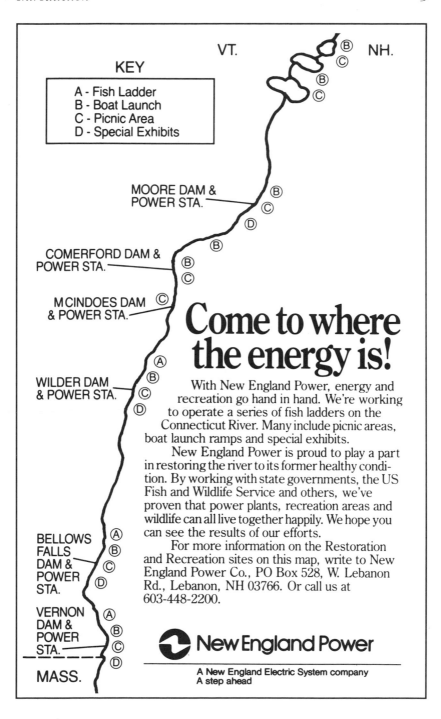

Acknowledgments

The Connecticut River Watershed Council would like to thank those individuals, organizations, and corporations who assisted in production of the first edition of *The Complete Boating Guide to the Connecticut River.* In addition, CRWC would like to acknowledge the following individuals, organizations, and corporations for their assistance and expertise in producing the second edition of *The Guide.*

Researchers, Reviewers, and Contributors:
Bradford Historical Society, Dave Carlson, Connecticut River Museum, Cornish Historical Society, John N. Critchley, Kenneth Curran, Peter Embarrato, James Fitch, Great Outdoors, Jim Hanrahan, Antonio Jocson, Betsy Katz, Lebanon Historical Society, Brenda Milkofsky, Barbara Moseley, George Moulton, New England Power, Northampton Historical Society, Northeast Utilities, Northfield Historical Society, Pfizer Central Research, John Ragonese, Rivers End Tackle, Dorothy Russell, Edith Royce Schade, Clyde Smith, Thetford Historical Society, Tom Whitehill.

CRWC Trustees:
Dave Engle, Tim Fowler, Sharon Francis, Astrid Hanzalzek, Erling Heistad, Cleve Kapala, Seth Kellogg, George Moulton, Mike Newbold, Charles Olchowski, Maython Phelps, Robert Pierce, Jean Richards, Peter Richardson, Jack Soper, Bud Twining, George Watkins, Martin Weiner.

CRWC Staff:
Richard Boyton, Geoff Dates, Henry S. Francis, Jr., Philip Klotz, Carol Ann Larocque, and special thanks to Sally Shepardson.

ENERGY ALLIANCE
NORTHEAST UTILITIES AND YOU

Working with our customers to conserve and reduce demand for energy.

Contents

MASSASCHUSETTS   156

CONNECTICUT   186

APPENDICES   235

Preface

Rising in the mountains near the Canadian border, the Connecticut River passes through ponds, down cataracts, between rock walls, around fields, over salt marshes, and then through Long Island Sound before finally washing into the Atlantic Ocean. At 410 miles long, draining 11,260 square miles of land, it is the longest and largest river in New England.

The Connecticut was one of the first rivers of the New World to be explored by Europeans. Its fertile valley nourished some of the most distinguished institutions of learning in the world. The mills along the River and its tributaries fired the Industrial Revolution. In spite of its beauty and history, however, the Connecticut River came to be known as the nation's "most beautifully landscaped sewer."

That is changing. Thanks to the Federal Clean Air and Water acts, and the efforts of thousands of individuals and of organizations like the Connecticut River Watershed Council (CWRC), most of the River is now clean enough for swimming.

The Connecticut River is an extraordinary resource. It provides water for drinking, irrigation, and industry. It generates power and is a natural route for transportation. It provides us with food and has the potential for providing much more. And the River offers almost unlimited recreational opportunities.

The Connecticut River Watershed Council is dedicated to the preservation, conservation, and management of the River as the most important natural resource in the region. We believe that the quality of life in New England is directly related to the quality of our environment, and, in particular, to the quality of the Connecticut River.

The CRWC produced this guide in hopes that more people will be able to enjoy the River and become involved in efforts to preserve it.

The Connecticut River Watershed Council, Inc.

The Connecticut River Watershed Council (CRWC) is a nonprofit, membership-supported organization dedicated to improving and protecting the water quality of the Connecticut River and its tributaries. The CRWC works with individuals, other organizations, corporations, and government agencies to resolve environmental problems and to plan for the future of the valley.

When the CRWC was established in 1952, the Connecticut River and many of its tributaries suffered from severe pollution. Through the efforts of many dedicated people, the River is experiencing a dramatic recovery.

The CRWC works to clean up those parts of the River that are still polluted. Some towns in the watershed still lack adequate municipal sewage treatment plants. Many towns and cities have antiquated combined storm-water and sanitary sewers that discharge untreated wastes into the River whenever it rains. Through public education, advocacy, research, and planning, the CRWC seeks to continue the process of cleaning the River.

The CRWC's land conservation efforts have protected several large areas in the watershed and many key resource lands, including several islands, wetlands, and valuable wildlife areas. Areas that are important for the return of the Atlantic salmon have been sites of the CRWC's protection efforts.

Public education, an important CRWC activity, can be both fun and informative. Each year the CRWC organizes a series of canoe trips along the River. Themes include history of the valley and bird life along the River. Other trips feature fishing, camping, and picnicking.

The CRWC is organized into four state councils representing the four states of the watershed. These councils are supported by professionally staffed offices in Lebanon, NH; Easthampton, MA; and Hartford, CT. We invite you to join the CRWC and help make the Connecticut River Valley a better place to live and to visit.

ESSEX ISLAND MARINA, INC.
ESSEX, CONNECTICUT
(203) 767-1267

How To Use This Guide

Each of the 29 River-segment descriptions in this book includes five different types of information about the River and surrounding country-side: maps, summary tables, boating facility tables, narrative descriptions, and sidebars.

Maps

Each segment begins with a map of the area of the River that is covered in the narrative description. The key to the symbols used in these maps is below. *Please note that the map scale varies.*

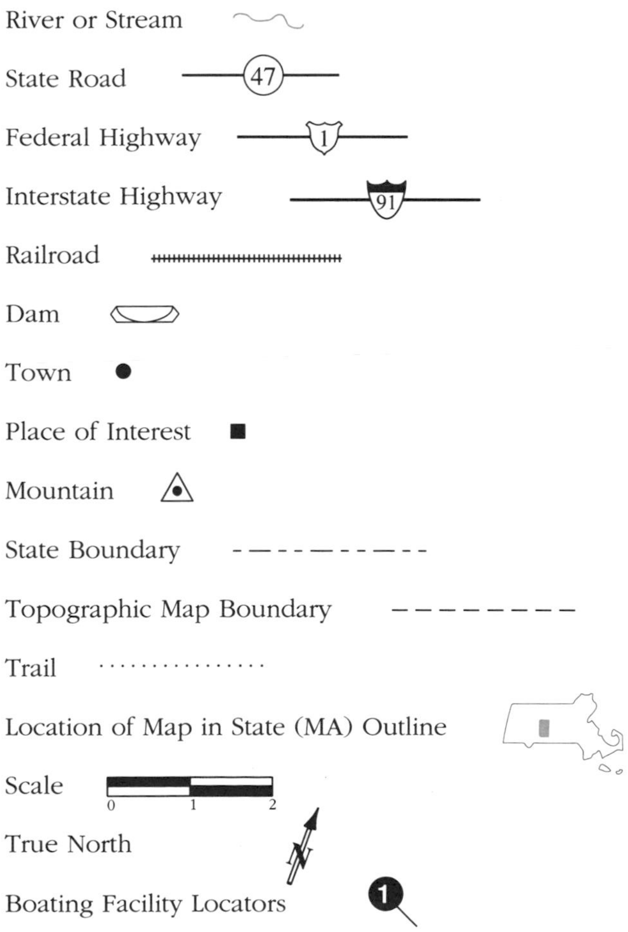

River or Stream

State Road   —(47)—

Federal Highway

Interstate Highway

Railroad

Dam

Town   ●

Place of Interest   ■

Mountain   △

State Boundary

Topographic Map Boundary

Trail

Location of Map in State (MA) Outline

Scale

True North

Boating Facility Locators

The maps included in this book are not designed to replace the National Oceanographic and Atmospheric Administration (NOAA) navigational charts that should be carried on board all boats operating from Hartford south or on Long Island Sound.

Summary Tables

The second part of every segment is the Summary Table.

EXAMPLE:

a. # East Haddam to Essex

b. MILES FROM MOUTH: 15.5-6.0 (9.5 mile span).

c. NAVIGABLE BY: All craft with drafts less than 15' and mast heights less than 81'.

d. DIFFICULTY: Flat water. (Beware of tides, winds, and boat wakes.)

e. PORTAGES: None.

f. CAMPING: Mile 12.5, Gillette Castle State Park, Hadlyme, CT (203) 526-2336.
Mile 11.5, Selden Neck State Park, Hadlyme, CT (203) 526-2336.

g. USGS: Deep River 7.5
Hamburg 7.5
Essex 7.5
Old Lyme 7.5

h. NOAA: Connecticut River:
Deep River to Bodkin Rock (#12377).
Long Island Sound to Deep River (#12375).

i. EMERGENCY HELP: East Haddam 911, VHF 1.6

KEY:

a. The section of the River that is being discussed.

b. Mileage reference points measured upriver from the Old Saybrook (CT) Lighthouse; length of the stretch discussed in the chapter.

c. The type of boats suitable for this section of the River; i.e., kayak, canoe, powerboat, sailboat.

d. The type of water conditions that can be expected; i.e.,

Flat water: smooth-surfaced water with slight current.

Quick water: faster running water with some riffles and small waves.

Class I-VI: Refers to the six difficulty classes from the *Safety Code of the American Whitewater Affiliation.* (See page 28 in the Boating Safety section for a description.)

e. Location (by mile reference number) of impassable obstacle such as a dam, falls, low bridge, etc.; side of River on which to portage; length of portage.

f. Location (by mile reference number) of established campsites; name of site; telephone number.

g. United States Geological Survey (USGS) maps for the region. Maps come in two scales: 7.5-minute series, and 15-minute series. Maps are being re-surveyed, so be sure you have the current editions from the

U.S. Geological Survey
Map Sales
Denver Federal Center
Box 25286
Denver, CO 80225
(303) 236-7477

h. National Oceanographic and Atmospheric Administration (NOAA) navigational charts for the area. Navigational charts are available from chandleries and sporting goods stores, and the

Distribution Branch N/CG-33
National Ocean Service
Riverdale, MD 20737-1199
(301) 436-6990

i. Who to call in emergencies: Where in effect, "911;" otherwise the
local police department numbers are listed. Many harbormasters in
the lower stretches of the river monitor VHF Channel 16.

Boating Facility Tables

The third part of each segment is the Boating Facility Table.

Boating Facilities and Services	Parking • Permit Required	Car-Topped Boat Access ☆	Ramp: Improved/Unimproved	Picnic Area/Water/Rest Rooms/Telephone	Gas/Diesel Fuel	Supplies/Food/Bait/Ice	Rent: Fishing Boats/Canoes/Kayaks	Repairs: Engines/Hulls/Propellers	MasterCard/VISA/American Express
1 Harbor One Marina Saybrook Point (203) 388-9208				WR T	G D	S I		E P	MV A
2 Saybrook Point Inn & Marina Saybrook Point (203) 388-0212				WR T	G D	SF IB		E P	MV A
3 Old Saybrook Town Ramp Sheffield Street (203) 388-2460	● ☆		I	TOWN RESIDENTS ONLY					

Information in these listings is provided by the facilities themselves. An asterisk (*) indicates that the facility did not respond to our most recent requests for information.

The Boating Facility Tables correspond directly to the Boating Facility
Locators appearing on the maps. Each marina, yacht club, and launching
ramp on the river section is identified in the table, with a phone number
where appropriate. The table also lists the services available at each
facility. Each launching ramp is identified as such, with the name of the
town, county, or state that maintains the ramp. If a ramp requires a permit,
the number to call for the permit is also listed. Where marinas or other
boating facilities are grouped closely together, locators will designate the
entire group, e.g. "9-13."

Narrative Descriptions

The third part of every River segment is the narrative description of what to look for and what to look out for while on the River. The descriptions go into detail about the conditions found on the River and the area through which the River flows. These descriptions are written north to south to follow the flow of the River. Suggested day-trips are also given where appropriate. For additional information about portages, access areas, and places of interest, we recommend that you read the narrative descriptions for the areas above and below the section of the River on which you will be boating.

The information in these descriptions was originally based on *The Connecticut River Guide* that was published by the CRWC in 1966. In 1986 the manuscript was updated and sent for further review to almost 100 individuals throughout the valley who have particular knowledge of and experience on various sections of the River. The result was the first edition of *The Complete Boating Guide to the Connecticut River*. This *Second Edition* is based on the first edition, but its contents have been completely re-checked and updated. In addition, Embassy Marine Publishing editors traveled the length of the Connecticut River by canoe and small outboard in the spring of 1990, gathering more on-site information.

Sidebars

The final part of each section is a sidebar or short article on history, geology, ecology, or whimsy that is not necessary for safe navigation but will hopefully add to your enjoyment of the River.

A Word of Caution

While we have prepared *The Complete Boating Guide to the Connecticut River, Second Edition* with as much care and in as much detail as possible, neither it nor any guide should be taken on blind faith. A river is in a constant state of flux. Sandbars will appear and disappear. Campgrounds and marinas will change. If during your travels on the River you note a change or some discrepancy in the text, or if you have additional information that would be useful to other boaters, please write to us so that we may include it in future editions of the *Boating Guide*.

Thank you.

Embassy Marine Publishing
P.O. Box 338
Essex, CT 06426

Boating Safety

Safety in boating is a matter of common sense. However, "common sense" is often more of a developed appreciation and understanding than an innate knowledge. It is for this reason that these guidelines and suggestions are offered. We hope that you will follow these suggestions until they become instinctive. No matter how experienced a boater you are, it is a good idea to review these guidelines from time to time.

Since boating on the Connecticut River can take the form of whitewater kayaking, coastal cruising, or anything in between, we have included two sets of boating-safety guidelines. Kayakers or canoeists should familiarize themselves with the American Whitewater Affiliation Safety Code, newly revised in 1989, and reprinted below with permission from the AWA. Sailors and powerboaters should review the U.S. Coast Guard Checklist For Safe Boating beginning on page 29. All boaters should file a float plan (page 32) whenever they head out.

Safety Code of the American Whitewater Affiliation

I. PERSONAL PREPAREDNESS AND RESPONSIBILTY

1. ***Be a competent swimmer,*** with the ability to handle yourself underwater.

2. ***Wear a lifejacket.*** A snugly fitting vest-type life preserver offers back and shoulder protection as well as the flotation needed to swim safely in whitewater.

3. ***Wear a solid, correctly fitted helmet*** when upsets are likely. This is essential in kayaks or covered canoes, and recommended for open canoeists using thigh straps, and rafters running steep drops.

4. ***Do not boat out of control.*** Your skills should be sufficient to stop or reach shore before reaching danger. Do not enter a rapid unless you are reasonably sure that you can run it safely or swim it without injury.

5. Whitewater rivers contain many hazards which are not always easily recognized. The following are the most frequent killers:

A. *High Water.* The river's speed and power increase tremendously as the flow increases, raising the difficulty of most rapids. Rescue becomes progressively harder as the water rises, adding to the danger. Floating debris and strainers make even an easy rapid quite hazardous. It is often misleading to judge the river level at the put in, since a small rise in a wide, shallow place will be multiplied many times where the river narrows. Use reliable gauge information whenever possible, and be aware that sun on snowpack, hard rain, and upstream dam releases may greatly increase the flow.

B. *Cold.* Cold drains your strength, and robs you of the ability to make sound decisions on matters affecting your survival. Cold water immersion, because of the initial shock and the rapid heat loss which follows, is especially dangerous. Dress appropriately for bad weather or sudden immersion in the water. When the water temperature is less than 50° F, a wetsuit or drysuit is essential for protection if you swim. Next best is wool or pile clothing under a waterproof shell. In this case, you should also carry waterproof matches and a change of clothing in a waterproof bag. Anyone experiencing uncontrollable shaking, loss of coordination, or difficulty speaking after prolonged exposure is hypothermic and needs immediate attention.

C. *Strainers.* Brush, fallen trees, bridge pilings, undercut rocks or anything else which allows river current to sweep through can pin boats and boaters against the obstacle. Water pressure on anything trapped this way can be overwhelming. Rescue is often difficult. Pinning may occur in fast current, with little or no whitewater to warn of the danger.

D. *Dams, Weirs, Ledges, Reversals, Holes, and Hydraulics.* When water drops over an obstacle, it curls back on itself, forming a strong upstream current which may be capable of holding a boat or a swimmer. Some holes make for excellent sport; others are proven killers. Paddlers who cannot recognize the differences should avoid all but the smallest holes. Hydraulics around man-made dams must be treated with the utmost respect, regardless of their height or the level of the river. Despite their seemingly benign appearance, they can create an almost escape-proof trap. The swimmer's only exit from the "drowning machine" is to dive below the surface when the downstream current is flowing beneath the reversal.

E. Broaching. When a boat is pushed sideways against a rock by strong current, it may collapse and wrap. This is especially dangerous to kayak and decked canoe paddlers; these boats will collapse and the combination of indestructible hulls and tight outfitting may create a deadly trap. Even without entrapment, releasing pinned boats can be extremely time-consuming and dangerous. To avoid pinning, throw your weight downstream towards the rock. This allows the current to slide harmlessly underneath the hull.

6. **Boating alone is discouraged.** The minimum party is three people or two craft.

7. **Have a frank knowledge of your boating ability,** and don't attempt rivers or rapids which lie beyond that ability.

   A. Develop the paddling skills and teamwork required to match the river you plan to boat. Most good paddlers develop skills gradually, and attempts to advance too quickly will compromise your safety and enjoyment.

   B. Be in good physical and mental condition, consistent with the difficulties which may be expected. Make adjustments for loss of skills due to age, health, or fitness. Any health limitation must be explained to your fellow paddlers prior to starting the trip.

8. **Be practiced in self-rescue,** including escape from an overturned craft. The eskimo roll is strongly recommended for decked boaters who run rapids of Class IV or greater, or who paddle in cold environmental conditions.

9. **Be trained in rescue skills, CPR, and first aid,** with special emphasis on recognizing and treating hypothermia. It may save a friend's life.

10. **Carry equipment needed for unexpected emergencies,** including footwear which will protect your feet when walking out, a throw rope, knife, whistle and waterproof matches. If you wear eyeglasses, tie them on and carry a spare pair on long trips. Bring cloth repair tape on short runs, and a full repair kit on isolated rivers. Do not wear bulky jackets, ponchos, heavy boots, or anything else which could reduce your ability to survive a swim.

11. **Despite the mutually supportive group structure described in this code, individual paddlers are ultimately responsible for their own safety, and must assume sole responsibility for the following:**

    A. The decision to participate on any trip. This includes an evaluation of the expected difficulty of the rapids under the conditions existing at the time of the put-in.

    B. The selection of appropriate equipment, including a boat design suited to their skills and the appropriate rescue and survival gear.

    C. The decision to scout any rapid and to run or portage according to their best judgement. Other members of the group may offer advice, but paddlers should resist pressure from anyone to paddle beyond their skills. It is also their responsibility to decide whether to pass up any walk-out or take-out opportunity.

    D. All trip participants should constantly evaluate their own and their group's safety, voicing their concerns when appropriate and following what they believe to be the best course of action. Paddlers are encouraged to speak with anyone whose actions on the water are dangerous, whether they are a part of their group or not.

II. BOAT AND EQUIPMENT PREPAREDNESS

1. **Test new and different equipment** under familiar conditions before relying on it for difficult runs. This is especially true when adopting a new boat design or outfitting system. Low volume craft may present additional hazards to inexperienced or poorly conditioned paddlers.

2. **Be sure your boat and gear are in good repair** before starting a trip. The more isolated and difficult the run, the more rigorous this inspection should be.

3. **Install flotation bags** in non-inflatable craft, securely fixed in each end, designed to displace as much water as possible. Inflatable boats should have multiple air chambers and be test-inflated before launching.

4. **Have strong, properly sized paddles or oars** for controlling your craft. Carry sufficient spares for the length and difficulty of the trip.

5. **Outfit your boat safely.** The ability to exit your boat quickly is an essential component of safety in rapids. It is your responsibility to see that there is absolutely nothing to cause entrapment when coming free of an upset craft. This includes:

   A. Spray covers which won't release reliably or which release prematurely.

   B. Boat outfitting too tight to allow a fast exit, especially in low volume kayaks or decked canoes. This includes low-hung thwarts in canoes lacking adequate clearance for your feet, and kayak footbraces which fail or allow your feet to become wedged under them.

   C. Inadequately supported decks which collapse on a paddler's legs when a decked boat is pinned by water pressure. Inadequate clearance with the deck because of your size or build.

   D. Loose ropes which cause entanglement. Beware of any length of loose line attached to a whitewater boat. All items must be tied tightly and excess line eliminated; painters, throw lines, and safety rope systems must be completely and effectively stored. Do not knot the end of a rope, as it can get caught in cracks between rocks.

6. **Provide ropes** which permit you to hold on to your craft so that it may be rescued. The following methods are recommended.

A. Kayaks and covered canoes should have grab loops of 1/4"+ rope or equivalent webbing sized to admit a normal sized hand. Stern painters are permissible if properly secured.

B. Open canoes should have securely anchored bow and stern painters consisting of 8-10 feet of 1/4"+ line. These must be secured in such a way that they are readily accessible, but cannot come loose accidentally. Grab loops are acceptable, but are more difficult to reach after an upset.

C. Rafts and dories may have taut perimeter lines threaded through the loops provided. Footholds should be designed so that a paddler's feet cannot be forced through them, causing entrapment. Flip lines should be carefully and reliably stowed.

7. **Know your craft's carrying capacity,** and how added loads affect boat handling in whitewater. Most rafts have a minimum crew size which can be added to on day trips or in easy rapids. Carrying more than two paddlers in an open canoe when running rapids is not recommended.

8. **Car top racks** must be strong and attach positively to the vehicle. Lash your boat to each crossbar, then tie the ends of the boats directly to the bumpers for added security. This arrangement should survive all but the most violent vehicle accident.

III. GROUP PREPAREDNESS AND RESPONSIBILITY

1. **Organization.** A river trip should be regarded as a common adventure by all participants, except on instructional or commercially guided trips as defined below. Participants share the responsibility for the conduct of the trip, and each participant is individually responsible for judging his or her own capabilities and for his or her own safety as the trip progresses. Participants are encouraged (but are not obligated) to offer advice and guidance for the independent consideration and judgement of others.

2. **River Conditions.** The group should have a reasonable knowledge of the difficulty of the run. Participants should

evaluate this information and adjust their plans accordingly. If the run is exploratory or no one is familiar with the river, maps and guidebooks, if available, should be examined. The group should secure accurate flow information; the more difficult the run, the more important this will be. Be aware of possible changes in river level and how this will affect the difficulty of the run. If the trip involves tidal stretches, secure appropriate information on tides.

3. **Group equipment should be suited to the difficulty of the river.** The group should always have a throw line available, and one line per boat is recommended on difficult runs. The list may include carabiners, prussick loops, first aid kit, flashlight, folding saw, fire starter, guidebooks, maps, food, extra clothing, and any other rescue or survival items suggested by conditions. Each item is not required on every run, and this list is not meant to be a substitute for good judgement.

4. **Keep the group compact,** but maintain sufficient spacing to avoid collisions. If the group is large, consider dividing into smaller groups or using the "Buddy System" as an additional safeguard. Space yourselves closely enough to permit good communication, but not so close as to interfere with one another in rapids.

    A.   The lead paddler sets the pace. When in front, do not get in over your head. Never run drops when you cannot see a clear route to the bottom or, for advanced paddlers, a sure route to the next eddy. When in doubt, stop and scout.

    B.   Keep track of all group members. Each boat keeps the one behind it in sight, stopping if necessary. Know how many people are in your group and take head counts regularly. No one should paddle ahead or walk out without first informing the group. Weak paddlers should stay at the center of a group, and not allow themselves to lag behind. If the group is large and contains a wide range of abilities, a designated "Sweep Boat" should bring up the rear.

    C.   Courtesy. On heavily used rivers, do not cut in front of a boater running a drop. Always look upstream before leaving eddies to run or play. Never enter a crowded drop or eddy when no room for you exists. Passing other groups in a rapid may be hazardous: it's often safer to wait upstream until the group ahead has passed.

5. **Float Plan.** If the trip is into a wilderness area or for an extended period, plans should be filed with a responsible person who will contact the authorities if you are overdue. It may be wise to establish checkpoints along the way where civilization could be contacted if necessary. Knowing the location of possible help and preplanning escape routes can speed rescue.

6. **Drugs.** The use of alcohol or mind-altering drugs before or during river trips is not recommended. It dulls reflexes, reduces decision-making ability, and may interfere with important survival reflexes.

7. **Instructional or Commercially Guided Trips.** In contrast to the common adventure trip format, in these trip formats a boating instructor or commercial guide assumes some of the responsibilities normally exercised by the group as a whole, as appropriate under the circumstances. These formats recognize that instructional or commercially guided trips may involve participants who lack significant experience in whitewater. However, as a participant acquires experience in whitewater, he or she takes on increasing responsibility for his or her own safety, in accordance with what he or she knows or should know as a result of that increased experience. Also, as in all trip formats, every participant must realize and assume the risks associated with the serious hazards of whitewater rivers. It is advisable for instructors and commercial guides to acquire trip or personal liability insurance.

   A. An "instructional trip" is characterized by a clear teacher/pupil relationship, where the primary purpose of the trip is to teach boating skills, and which is conducted for a fee.

   B. A "commercially guided trip" is characterized by a licensed, professional guide conducting trips for a fee.

IV. GUIDELINES FOR RIVER RESCUE

1. **Recover from an upset with an eskimo roll** whenever possible. Evacuate your boat immediately if there is imminent

danger of being trapped against rocks, brush, or any other kind of strainer.

2. **If you swim, hold on to your boat.** It has much flotation and is easy for rescuers to spot. Get to the upstream end so that you cannot be crushed between a rock and your boat by the force of the current. Persons with good balance may be able to climb on top of a swamped kayak or flipped raft and paddle to shore.

3. **Release your craft if this will improve your chances,** especially if the water is cold or dangerous rapids lie ahead. Actively attempt self-rescue whenever possible by swimming for safety. Be prepared to assist others who may come to your aid.

   A. When swimming in shallow or obstructed rapids, lie on your back *with feet held high* and pointed downstream. Do not attempt to stand in fast moving water; if your foot wedges on the bottom, fast water will push you under and keep you there. Get to slow or very shallow water before attempting to stand or walk. Look ahead! Avoid possible pinning situations including undercut rocks, strainers, downed trees, holes, and other dangers by swimming away from them.

   B. If the rapids are deep and powerful, roll over onto your stomach and swim aggressively for shore. Watch for eddies and slackwater and use them to get out of the current. Strong swimmers can effect a powerful upstream ferry and get to shore fast. If the shores are obstructed with strainers or undercut rocks, however, it is safer to "ride the rapid out" until a safer escape can be found.

4. **If others spill and swim, go after the people first.** Rescue boats and equipment only if this can be done safely. While participants are encouraged (but not obligated) to assist one another to the best of their ability, they should do so only if they can, in their judgment, do so safely. The first duty of a rescuer is not to compound the problem by becoming another victim.

5. **The use of rescue lines requires training;** uninformed use may cause injury. Never tie yourself into either end of a line without a reliable quick-release system. Have a knife handy to deal with unexpected entanglement. Learn to place set lines

effectively, to throw accurately, to belay effectively, and to properly handle a rope thrown to you.

6. **When reviving a drowning victim,** be aware that cold water may greatly extend survival time underwater. Victims of hypothermia may have depressed vital signs so they look and feel dead. Don't give up; continue CPR for as long as possible without compromising safety.

V. UNIVERSAL RIVER SIGNALS

STOP: Potential hazard ahead. Wait for "all clear" signal before proceeding, or scout ahead. Form a horizontal bar with your outstretched arms. Those seeing the signal should pass it back to others in the party.

HELP/EMERGENCY: Assist the signaller as quickly as possible. Give three long blasts on a police whistle while waving a paddle, helmet or life vest over your head. If a whistle is not available, use the visual signal alone. A whistle is best carried on a lanyard attached to your life vest.

ALL CLEAR: Come ahead (in the absence of other directions proceed down the center). Form a vertical bar with your paddle or one arm held high above your head. Paddle blade should be turned flat for maximum visibility. To signal direction or a preferred course through a rapid around obstruction, lower the previously vertical "all clear" by 45 degrees toward the side of the river with the preferred route. Never point toward the obstacle you wish to avoid.

VI. INTERNATIONAL SCALE OF RIVER DIFFICULTY

This is the American version of a rating system used to compare river difficulty throughout the world. This system is not exact; rivers do not always fit easily into one category, and regional or individual interpretations may cause misunderstandings. It is no substitute for a guidebook or accurate first-hand descriptions of a run.

Paddlers attempting difficult runs in an unfamiliar area should act cautiously until they get a feel for the way the scale is interpreted locally. River difficulty may change each year due to fluctuations in water level, downed trees, geological disturbances, or bad weather. Stay alert for unexpected problems!

As river difficulty increases, the danger to swimming paddlers becomes more severe. As rapids become longer and more continuous, the challenge increases. There is a difference between running an occasional Class IV rapid and dealing with an entire river of this category. Allow an extra margin of safety between skills and river ratings when the water is cold or if the river itself is remote and inaccessible.

The Six Difficulty Classes

Class I: Easy. Fast moving water with riffles and small waves. Few obstructions, all obvious and easily missed with little training. Risk to swimmers is slight; self-rescue is easy.

Class II: Novice. Straightforward rapids with wide, clear channels which are evident without scouting. Occasional maneuvering may be required, but rocks and medium-sized waves are easily missed by trained paddlers. Swimmers are seldom injured and group assistance, while helpful, is seldom needed.

Class III: Intermediate. Rapids with moderate, irregular waves which may be difficult to avoid and which can swamp an open canoe. Complex maneuvers in fast current and good boat control in tight passages or around ledges are often required; large waves or strainers may be present but are easily avoided. Strong eddies and powerful current effects can be found, particularly on large-volume rivers. Scouting is advisable for inexperienced parties. Injuries while swimming are rare; self-rescue is usually easy but group assistance may be required to avoid long swims.

Class IV: Advanced. Intense, powerful but predictable rapids requiring precise boat handling in turbulent water. It may feature large, unavoidable waves and holes or constricted passages demanding fast maneuvers under pressure. A fast, reliable eddy turn may be needed to initiate maneuvers, scout rapids, or rest. Rapids may require "must" moves above dangerous hazards. Scouting is necessary the first time down. Risk of injury to swimmers is moderate to high, and water conditions may make self-rescue difficult. Group assistance for rescue is often essential but requires practiced skills. A strong eskimo roll is highly recommended.

Class V: Expert. Extremely long, obstructed, or very violent rapids which expose a paddler to above average endangerment. Drops may contain large, unavoidable waves and holds or steep, congested chutes with complex, demanding routes. Rapids may continue for long distances between pools, demanding a high level of fitness. What eddies exist may be small, turbulent, or difficult to reach. At the high end of the scale, several of these factors may be combined. Scouting is mandatory but often difficult. Swims are dangerous, and rescue is difficult even for experts. A very reliable eskimo roll, proper equipment, extensive experience, and practiced rescue skills are essential for survival.

Class VI: Extreme. One grade more difficult than Class V. These runs often exemplify the extremes of difficulty, unpredictability and danger. The consequences of errors are very severe and rescue may be impossible. For teams of experts only, at favorable water levels, after close personal inspection and taking all precautions. This class does *not* represent drops thought to be unrunnable, but may include rapids which are only occasionally run.

United States Coast Guard Checklist for Safe Boating

BE EDUCATED AND PREPARED

- THE OVERWHELMING MAJORITY OF BOAT OPERATORS THAT HAVE FATAL ACCIDENTS HAVE NEVER TAKEN A SAFE BOATING COURSE. Call the toll-free "Courseline" (1-800-336-2628) for information on courses available in your locality.

- Carry all safety equipment required by Federal and State law. Federal requirements are discussed in the pamphlet: "Federal Requirements for Recreational Boats," which you can get by writing to the U.S. Coast Guard, Office of Navigation Safety & Waterway Services, Washington, DC 20593-0001. Your State Boating Law Administrator can tell you if your State has any additional requirements. Also recommended:

—a first aid kit	—paddles or oars
—a manual pump or bailer	—anchor and line
—a transistor radio	—drinking water
—extra fuel	—distress flares (now a requirement in many areas)

● Have a Coast Guard Auxiliary Courtesy Marine Examination–a free inspection to see if you are complying with Federal and State safety requirements. The inspection is strictly confidential. Call the "Courseline" to contact a local courtesy examiner.

● Familiarize yourself and your crew with distress signals and emergency procedures. Practice putting on Personal Flotation Devices (PFDs).

AVOID FIRES AND EXPLOSIONS

● Handle volatile fuels carefully.
● Check with your owner's manual for proper fuel and ventilation system maintenance.
● Test and inspect for fuel leaks periodically.
● Heed regulations concerning fire extinguishers and keep them in good condition.
● Refueling is dangerous if safety precautions are not observed:
  – Fill all portable tanks *on the dock.*
  – Moor boat securely.
  – Extinguish cigarettes and all flames on boat and turn off all engines and electrical equipment.
  – Close all window and door openings in galley.
  – Keep hose nozzle grounded.
  – Wipe up all gasoline or oil spillage.
  – Keep fire extinguisher handy.
  – Ventilate engine and fuel compartment and check for fumes and gas odors.
  – Use your bilge blower for at least four minutes before starting an inboard engine.

BEFORE GETTING UNDERWAY

● LEAVE A FLOAT PLAN WITH SOMEONE **(See page 32)**.

● DISTRIBUTE WEIGHT PROPERLY, especially if you have a small boat. Do not overload. Follow the limit on the capacity plate. *Load low and spread the load around.*

WHILE UNDERWAY

● BE ESPECIALLY CAREFUL IF YOU HAVE A SMALL BOAT (a boat 20' or under). *The overwhelming majority of capsizings occur on small boats because of sudden weight shifts. Any small boat can be "tippy."*

● The Coast Guard recommends that PFDs be worn by children and non-swimmers at all times. *Everyone should wear them if conditions become hazardous.* THE MOST COMMON CAUSE OF BOATING ACCIDENT DEATHS IS DROWNING AND HYPOTHERMIA – SITUATIONS WHERE THE VICTIM MIGHT HAVE SURVIVED BY WEARING A PFD.

● DO NOT OPERATE A BOAT IF *INTOXICATED, FATIGUED, OR STRESSED.* These human factors cause over 50 percent of all boating accidents. Remember that reaction time is much slower after being out in the marine environment for a few hours.

● KEEP A GOOD LOOKOUT. Failure to do so causes most collisions. You need a second person to act as lookout if towing a skier.

● TRAVEL AT SAFE SPEEDS. Give swimmers, skiers, and divers a wide berth.

● OBEY State and Federal laws, local laws, and "Rules of the Road."

● RESPECT BAD WEATHER. Try to get to shore if the weather turns bad. NOAA weather is heard on radios with a "weather band" or on special weather radios on high-band FM frequencies 162.40 to 162.55 MHz. Some weather radios turn on automatically if a warning is broadcast. You can get a list of weather radio manufacturers by writing to: National Weather Service (Attn: W/OM 15X2), NOAA, Silver Spring, MD 20910. You can also get the National Weather Service boating forecast phone number from information.

IF YOU GET INTO TROUBLE

Radio for help. Use the emergency VHF channel 16 (156.8 MHz) if in trouble. (The Coast Guard also monitors CB channel 9 *whenever resources permit monitoring;* VHF channel 16 is monitored constantly.)

Everyone should wear PFDs if conditions become hazardous.

In most capsizings, chances of survival and being found are better if you *stay with the boat* (even if you are a good swimmer). *In cold water, climb onto a capsized boat or huddle together to prevent hypothermia.* 🔅

Float Plan

Complete this page before going boating and leave it with a reliable person who can be depended upon to notify the Coast Guard or other rescue organization should you not return as scheduled. Do not file this plan with the Coast Guard.

1. Name of person reporting:_____ Phone:_____
2. Type of boat:_____ Color:_____
   Trim:_____ Registration No.:_____
   Length:_____ Name:_____ Make:_____
   Other information:_____
3. Persons aboard: Name, Address, Telephone No.:

   _____

   _____

   _____

4. Engine type:_____ H.P.:_____
   No. of engines:_____ Fuel Capacity:_____
5. Survival equipment: (Check as appropriate)
   PFDs_____ Flares_____ Mirror_____ Smoke signals_____
   Flashlight____ Food_____ Paddles____ Water_____
   Anchor_____ Raft or dinghy_____
   Other_____
6. Radio: Type:_____ Frequencies:_____
7. Trip expectations: Leaving time_____
   Starting location:_____
   Finishing location:_____
   Expect to return by:_____
   Return no later than:_____
8. Any other pertinent information:_____
9. Color, make, name of car:_____
   License: Car:_____ Trailer:_____
   Where parked:_____
10. If not returned by (time)_____
    CALL:_____ Phone:_____
    _____ Phone:_____
    _____ Phone:_____

Copy this form as needed.

First Aid

The following is provided as a reference only. If the situation is serious, take the victim to a hospital immediately.

1. BREATHING DIFFICULTY

IF THERE IS NO RESPONSE, TILT THE VICTIM'S HEAD, CHIN POINTING UP. Place one hand under the victim's neck and gently lift. At the same time, push with the other hand on the victim's forehead. This will move the tongue from the back of the throat to open the airway.

IMMEDIATELY LOOK, LISTEN, AND FEEL FOR AIR. While maintaining the backward head tilt position, place your cheek and ear close to the victim's mouth and nose. Look for the chest to rise and fall while you listen and feel for the return of air. Check for about 5 seconds.

IF THE VICTIM IS NOT BREATHING, GIVE FOUR QUICK BREATHS. Maintain the backward head tilt, pinch the victim's nose with the hand that is on the victim's forehead to prevent leakage of air; open your mouth wide, take a deep breath, seal your mouth around the victim's mouth, and blow into the victim's mouth with four quick but full breaths as fast as you can. When blowing, use only enough time between breaths to lift your head slightly for better inhalation. For an infant, give gentle puffs and blow through the mouth and nose and do not tilt the head back as far as an adult. If you do not get an air exchange when you blow, reposition the head and try again.

AGAIN, LOOK, LISTEN, AND FEEL FOR AIR EXCHANGE.

IF THERE IS STILL NO BREATHING, CHANGE RATE TO ONE BREATH EVERY 5 SECONDS FOR AN ADULT.

FOR AN INFANT, GIVE ONE GENTLE PUFF EVERY 3 SECONDS.

MOUTH TO NOSE METHOD. The mouth to nose method can be used with the sequence described above instead of the mouth to mouth method. Maintain the backward head tilt position with the hand on the victim's forehead. Remove the hand from under the neck and close the victim's mouth. Blow into the victim's nose. Open the victim's mouth for the look, listen, and feel step.

FIRST AID FOR CHOKING

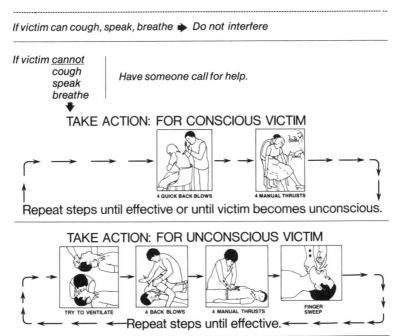

If victim can cough, speak, breathe ➡ Do not interfere

If victim <u>cannot</u>
    cough | Have someone call for help.
    speak |
    breathe |
    ⬇

TAKE ACTION: FOR CONSCIOUS VICTIM

4 QUICK BACK BLOWS   4 MANUAL THRUSTS

Repeat steps until effective or until victim becomes unconscious.

TAKE ACTION: FOR UNCONSCIOUS VICTIM

TRY TO VENTILATE   4 BACK BLOWS   4 MANUAL THRUSTS   FINGER SWEEP

Repeat steps until effective.

Continue artificial ventilation or CPR, as indicated.

2. BLEEDING

Bleeding may be stopped by applying firm pressure directly over the wound to form clotting or by digital pressure on a pressure point in the affected arm or leg or both.

3. POISONING

First Aid for Conscious Victim of Poisoning

1) Dilute the poison by having the victim drink a glass of water or milk, if the victim is conscious and not having convulsions. Discontinue dilution if it makes the victim nauseous.

2) Save the label or container of the suspected poison for identification. If the victim vomits, save a sample of the vomited material for analysis.

3) Seek medical assistance by calling the poison control center or a physician. You should post the poison control center number for your region on your telephone. If you do not have the number, dial O (operator) or 911.

4) If the victim becomes unconscious, keep his or her airway open. Give artificial respiration or cardiopulmonary resuscitation (CPR), if indicated. Call an emergency squad as soon as possible. (Also see "First Aid for Unconscious Victim.")

First Aid for Unconscious Victim of Poisoning
1) Maintain an open airway.
2) Call for an emergency squad as soon as possible.
3) Administer artificial respiration and CPR, if indicated.
4) Save the container of the suspected poison.
5) If the patient has vomited, save a sample of the vomited material.
6) Do not give fluids to an unconscious person.
7) Do not induce vomiting in an unconscious person. If the victim is vomiting, position him or her on his or her side and turn the person's head so that the material drains out of the mouth.

4. ANIMAL BITES

Wash the wound thoroughly, using a solution of soap and water. Rinse with clean running water. Apply sterile dressing. Always consult a physician at once. Confine animal to escapeproof quarters. Notify the police.

5. BRUISES

Apply ice bag or cold pack. If skin is broken, treat as a minor cut.

6. BURNS AND SCALDS

For burns of limited extent: Apply cold water. Cover with sterile dressing. For extensive burns: Treat for shock. Remove loose clothing. Do not remove clothing which sticks to burned area. Consult a physician. Never apply oil, butter, or any preparation to a burn. If burn covers a considerable area or if fever or blisters develop, see a physician.

7. CUTS

Wash with soap and water. Wash away from–not into–the cut. Apply direct pressure over cut with sterile gauze until bleeding stops. Apply antibacterial ointment and sterile dressing.

8. EYES

Foreign bodies: Remove only those foreign bodies lying on the surface of the eye. Lift off with the corner of a clean handkerchief or flush eye with water, using eye dropper or bulb syringe. Do not rub eye. Never remove anything embedded in eyeball. Consult physician.

9. FAINTING

Keep person lying down with head slightly lowered. Loosen any tight clothing about neck. If person does not respond within a short time, summon a physician.

10. FRACTURES

Deformity of injured part usually means fracture. If fracture is suspected, do not attempt to move injured person. Call physician at once. Treat for shock.

11. FROSTBITE AND CHILLS

Handle gently to avoid injury. Bring person into warm room and give warm drink. Immerse body part in lukewarm but not hot water or gently wrap in warm blankets. Do not rub or expose to stove or fire, or put in hot water. Such procedures may cause serious permanent damage.

12. HEAT CRAMPS

Symptoms: Cramps in muscles of abdomen and extremities. Treatment: Same as for heat exhaustion.

13. HEAT EXHAUSTION

Symptoms: Cool, clammy skin with body temperature about normal or below. Treatment: Keep person lying down with head lowered. If conscious, give saltwater solution to drink (1 teaspoon of salt to 1 glass of water) in small amounts at frequent intervals.

14. HEAT STROKE

Symptoms: Hot, dry skin and extremely high body temperature. Treatment: Repeatedly sponge bare skin with cool water or rubbing alcohol, or apply cold packs or place person in a tub of cold water (do not add ice) until body temperature is sufficiently lowered. Do not give stimulants. Consult a physician immediately.

15. INSECT BITES

Remove stinger if present. Apply cold applications and soothing lotions, such as calamine. If person has history of allergic reactions to insect bites, get him or her to a physician at once.

16. POISON IVY

Wash exposed area well with naphtha (yellow) soap. Do not use a brush or other rough material. Then use rubbing alcohol, if available.

Apply calamine lotion. If area spreads, swells, or forms large blisters, see a physician.

17. PUNCTURE WOUNDS
Encourage bleeding by mild pressure around the wound. Treat the same as cuts. Always see a physician. A tetanus injection is usually necessary.

18. SCRAPES
Wash with soap and water. Blot dry and treat the same as cuts. If scrape is deep and dirty, see a physician.

19. SHOCK
Keep person lying down. Cover only enough to prevent body heat loss. Get medical help.

20. SPLINTERS
Wash area with soap and water. Sterilize needle point by passing it through a flame and use it to tease out splinter. Apply antibacterial ointment and sterile dressing.

21. SPRAINS
Elevate injured part to minimize swelling and apply ice bags or cold cloths immediately after injury. Cold application of Epsom salts may be repeated every two hours. If swelling is pronounced, do not attempt to use injured part until seen by a physician.

22. STRAINS
Apply heating pad or heat lamp, then warm, wet application to affected area. Bed rest is indicated. If strained back, place board under the mattress for firm support.

23. UNCONSCIOUSNESS
Never attempt to give anything by mouth. Never attempt to induce vomiting. Place patient lying on side with head on arm. Loosen tight clothing; maintain body heat with blanket. Summon a physician at once. Be sure patient is breathing. If not, give artificial respiration.

Illustrations reprinted with permission of the American Red Cross.

The River

The Geology of the Valley

The geologic history of the Connecticut River Valley reflects the history of the Earth itself. It all began about 4.6 billion years ago with the formation of the Earth – at least that is the current belief of geologists. More recently – some 400 to 250 million years ago – the Earth went through another traumatic experience when the continents of North America, South America, Africa, and Europe bumped into each other, forming the supercontinent known as Pangaea. This collision was not a sudden event, as the continents moved only a few inches each year. But the severity of the collision was such that it created a range of mountains 5 to 7 miles high. These were the ancient Appalachian Mountains. The backbone of the Appalachian Mountains gives the Connecticut River Valley its basic shape and its north-south orientation.

About 200 million years ago the supercontinent started to split apart. Several enormous cracks formed before the continents finally pulled apart and the oceans flowed in to complete the separation. One of the largest of these cracks gave the Connecticut River Valley its second most recognizable feature, the wide central lowland of the Pioneer Valley.

For a few million years, while the central lowland was slowly being filled and leveled with sediment from the rest of the basin, New England had a subtropical climate. Locally, lush vegetation covered areas of the countryside, and dinosaurs roamed the land, leaving their tracks in the soft brown mud at Rocky Hill, CT, and Hadley, MA. But about 65 million years ago the dinosaurs had become extinct. We still are not certain why. As millions of years passed, erosion gradually wore away the once lofty Appalachians, leaving only their roots, now exposed at the surface.

About 1.5 million years ago a series of ice ages began. Several continental ice sheets moved south across New England. These glaciers, the last of which melted about 17,000 years ago, had a profound effect on the Connecticut River Valley. These glaciers were up to 2 miles thick and at one time covered all of eastern Canada and most of the northern United States. So much water was locked up in the ice sheets that the oceans dropped by more than 300 feet.

As the glaciers moved south, they greatly accelerated the slow erosion of the landscape. The glaciers acted like a phalanx of the world's biggest bulldozers, smoothing off mountains, filling in and deepening valleys, dragging boulders hundreds of miles, and spreading debris (till).

And then they stopped. The climate began to warm, and the glaciers melted. At the southern end of the glacier, an enormous pile of debris (the terminal moraine) was left as the glacier receded. This debris pile and the bedrock beneath it is known as Long Island. As the glacier melted and haltingly crept back north, it left other (recessional) moraines and many meltwater sand and gravel deposits along the way. One of the most significant was a delta formed in the vicinity of Cromwell, CT.

The local topography of Cromwell was such that the delta formed a natural dam across the entire drainage basin, trapped the meltwater behind it, and created a lake that extended all the way to Lyme, NH. Lake Hitchcock, as it is now called, was 170 miles long and up to 8 miles wide. For the few thousand years that it existed, the annual winter dry season and summer runoff deposited layer after layer of fine and slightly coarser sediment (varved deposits), slowly leveling the bottom of the lake.

Eventually, the dam at Cromwell eroded. Lake Hitchcock was drained, leaving what is now the Connecticut River Valley. Where the lake bed had been lay a broad and fertile plain. The plain was further leveled and enriched by periodic flooding. This process created the rich agricultural fields of the Pioneer Valley that first attracted the American colonists. Many believe that the glaciers were also responsible for the sandbar at the River's mouth. But in fact, it is the prevailing winds, currents, and tides that created the troublesome sandbar at Old Saybrook.

Where the Connecticut River flowed through mountainous areas, such as in the upper valley, it was confined by the bedrock and took the fastest route to the sea. This created a fairly narrow and straight river. In areas where the terrain was more level, such as the Pioneer Valley, the current was slower and more easily diverted from its straight path. Shallow loops, or meanders, were formed. Once started, these loops had a tendency to become more and more exaggerated. Eventually the meanders doubled back on themselves, cutting short the loop and leaving an island and an "oxbow lake." There are several excellent examples of oxbows on the Connecticut River, most notably at Wethersfield, CT; Northampton, MA; and North Haverhill, NH.

In the last 300 years another force has made a profound impact on the geology of the Connecticut River Valley. In that time, man has carved roads and built dikes. We have blasted away mountains and dammed the River. But 300 years on man's calendar is but a few seconds of the geologic year. Nevertheless, the combined effects of man's constructive and destructive energies coupled with a possible rapid rise in the level of the ocean in the next several decades because of the "greenhouse effect" suggests that our geologic environment is presently changing as fast as, possibly faster than, it ever has before.

Thanks to Sidney Quarrier, Geologist with the Connecticut Department of Environmental Protection, for his help in compiling this article.

The History of the Valley

The first evidence of human occupation of the Connecticut River Valley dates from 10,000 years ago. Little is known of these Paleo-Indians other than that they were big game hunters. As the climate and associated flora and fauna changed, the lives of the humans also changed. While still nomadic, the native Americans exploited the increasingly diverse plant and animal resources of the area. About 1,000 years ago, the Indians of southern New England began to cultivate corn, beans, and squash.

The advent of horticulture brought a semipermanent lifestyle. Villages were established along rivers and used the waterways for food, trade,and transportation. From here they would make trips to hunt, fish, gather raw materials for tools and utensils, and trade with other Indian groups. Local Indians were still practicing this seminomadic lifestyle when European settlers first began to trade in and occupy the Connecticut River Valley.

The Dutch explorer Adriaen Block was the first European to explore the River, sailing to the head of navigation at the Enfield Rapids in 1614. Some years later, the Dutch established trading posts at Saybrook and Hartford. To satisfy the demand for furs, Europeans traded metal and cloth for beaver, fox, and mink.

The first English settlers sailed from Massachusetts to Windsor in 1633. Other settlements were established in Wethersfield in 1634 and in Saybrook in 1635. The next year Thomas Hooker settled Hartford and William Pynchon came to Agawam, now Springfield. Only three years after his arrival, Hooker promulgated the Fundamental Orders, the first formal adoption in the American colonies of the principles of self-government based on "the free consent of the people." The English and the Dutch had conflicting claims on the valley, but in 1654 the Dutch were ousted and the English took complete control.

In the ensuing years the various settlements expanded: Saybrook soon encompassed Lyme, Essex, Westbrook, Deep River, and Chester; from Hartford and Wethersfield, people moved downriver to Cromwell, Middletown, and the Haddams; from Springfield, groups moved northward to Northampton, Hadley, Deerfield, and Greenfield. The northernmost settlements saw frequent Indian attacks that led to King Philip's War in 1675, and the virtual annihilation of the Indians in southern New England.

The end of the 17th century brought peace and prosperity to the lower River valley. The upper valley, however, saw numerous conflicts between English settlers and the Indians, who were allied with the French in Canada. The most famous conflict was the Deerfield Massacre of 1704.

The second quarter of the 18th century saw the expansion of the settlements in the upper valley. Settlements initially took the form of forts:

Fort Dummer near Brattleboro in 1725, Bellows Falls in 1735, and four years later, Rockingham and Westminster. Charlestown, NH was the site of the famous Fort No. 4 where a French and Indian attack was repulsed in 1747. It was also to Fort No. 4 that Robert Rogers returned with his Rangers after a punitive raid on the St. Francis Indians of Quebec.

In the 1760s the so-called New Hampshire grants opened up much of the land on both sides of the River, leading to the settlement of Lebanon, Hanover, and Lyme on the eastern side, and Windsor, Springfield, and St. Johnsbury in the west. Vermont, as such, did not then exist. There were numerous conflicting jurisdictional claims by Massachusetts, New Hampshire, and New York in which Ethan Allen and the Green Mountain Boys played a leading role. These differences were not resolved until after the Revolutionary War, with the admission of Vermont as the 14th state of the Union. In fact, boundary disputes between Vermont and New Hampshire continued until 1933, when the Supreme Court set markers on the Vermont side of the River so that New Hampshire owned the River and had to maintain the bridges across it. Historical precedent for the decision came from King George III, who had ruled that all lands as far as the "western banks of the River Connecticut" belonged to New Hampshire.

The lower valley was little affected by the wars and problems of the upper valley. Prosperity and improving the quality of life were important to the towns along the River in Massachusetts and Connecticut. Agriculture was the main occupation, rivaled only by shipbuilding in towns south of Windsor, CT. Middletown was the most important port in Connecticut and a leading shipping center for the West Indies trade. With a population of 5,564, it was the largest and wealthiest town on the River. In 1773 heavy River trade prompted the Connecticut General Assembly to mark the River channels and sandbars, paid for with money from a lottery.

There was little military action in the Connecticut River Valley during the American Revolution, but privateers from Hartford, Middletown, East Haddam, and Essex helped by preying on British shipping. The first American-built warship, the *Oliver Cromwell*, was built in Essex. The Connecticut River Valley provided supplies and provisions to the revolutionary cause. Hartford's Jeremiah Wadsworth had hundreds of tons of food and ammunition transported to Washington's troops at Valley Forge. In 1771, Washington and Rochambeau of France met at Wethersfield to plan the campaign that culminated in the surrender of Cornwallis at Yorktown. After the Revolution, men such as General Henry Knox of Springfield, Chief Justice Oliver Ellsworth of Windsor, lexicographer Noah Webster of Hartford, the Wolcotts, and others from the River valley continued to play influential roles in the development of the United States.

In 1786, economically displaced farmers led by Daniel Shays of Pelham, MA, rebelled against the Massachusetts court, demanding the restructuring of the tax system. On February 2, 1787, Shays fled to safety in Vermont, with the death penalty awaiting his return to Massachusetts. The call for a national constitutional convention and the establishment of a strong central government were in part a reaction to Shay's Rebellion and the states' inability to deal with such cases individually.

General prosperity followed until 1806 when President Jefferson imposed an international trade embargo that spelled financial disaster for many of the seafaring towns of the lower valley. The only encounter of the War of 1812 to take place along the River was the 1814 British raid on Essex, CT where some 23 ships were burned.

The Connecticut River Valley can be called the birthplace of the Industrial Revolution in America. By the early 19th century there were scores of small factories through the valley powered by the flowing water of the Connecticut River and its tributaries. However, the valley's most important contribution was the development of the concept of interchangeable parts. This technological breakthrough led to the machine-tool and small-arms industries of Middletown and Hartford in Connecticut, of Springfield in Massachusetts, and of Windsor in Vermont. Holyoke, MA has the distinction of being the first planned industrial community in the United States. In 1849 a dam was constructed across the River to divert the water into three canals. Mills along the canals used the water to generate mechanical power, or as process water.

It was during these years that the valley became home to numerous educational institutions. By 1810 Dartmouth College (chartered in 1769) in Hanover, NH had become one of the leading colleges in the country. The Hartford School for the Deaf, the oldest school for the disabled in the United States, was founded in 1817. Amherst College in Massachusetts followed in 1821, Trinity College in Hartford in 1823, and Wesleyan in Middletown in 1830. Mount Holyoke opened in 1837 as a seminary for women and became one of the outstanding colleges of the region. Smith College in Northampton, MA was founded in 1873.

As early as 1787, John Fitch of South Windsor, CT had successfully operated a steam-powered boat. Five years later, Samuel Morey ran a steamboat from Orford, NH to Fairlee, VT. In 1822, regularly scheduled steamboat service between Hartford and New York was inaugurated, with stops at intervening towns. The building of the Windsor Locks Canal in 1829 permitted steamboat service between Hartford and Springfield. The railroads, however, were fierce competition for the steamboats, and most steamboat runs were abandoned after the arrival of the rails. The Hartford-to-New York steamboat run was the last to go, in 1931.

New England as a whole, and with it the Connecticut River Valley, prospered toward the end of the 19th century. The greatly expanded cities were graced with fine public buildings, parks, churches, libraries, theaters, and museums. There were many prominent literary figures living in the valley: Lydia Sigourney, Mark Twain, and Harriet Beecher Stowe in Hartford; Samuel Bowles in Springfield; Emily Dickinson in Amherst; Edward Bellamy in Chicopee; Henry James in Northampton; Rudyard Kipling in Brattleboro. The artists Thomas Cole and Frederick Church came from Hartford. Augustus Saint-Gaudens, perhaps America's foremost sculptor, was part of a colony of artists in Cornish, NH. In the early 1900s, an artists' colony of American Impressionists thrived in Old Lyme, CT; many works can still be seen in the Florence Griswold Museum there. Famed actor and playwright, William Gillette, built his stone castle on a bluff overlooking the River in Hadlyme, CT. Middletown, Old Lyme, and Cornish were all home to Woodrow Wilson, and it was to Northampton that Calvin Coolidge returned at the end of his Presidency.

Unfortunately, the economic prosperity of the present century was accompanied by the gross neglect and abuse of the River. Raw sewage and industrial wastes were dumped into the River. Pollution had a severe impact on the already decimated fish population. Riverbanks in urban areas were disfigured with rubbish dumps and broken-down factories. The floodplain development radically changed the dynamics of the River, greatly increasing the severity of the floods of 1927, 1936, and the hurricane of 1938, as well as several floods in more recent years.

In the last 30 years, however, a new awareness of the importance of the River has developed. The River is now being recognized as an economic resource, but, more important, as an amenity to life that should be valued for its beauty, environmental uniqueness, and recreational opportunities. Cities such as Springfield, Hartford, and Middletown have made considerable strides in reclaiming their riverfronts. With the success achieved so far in the cleaning and preservation of the River, we can look optimistically, if cautiously, to the future. 🏞

Saint-Gaudens National Historic Site
Saint-Gaudens Rd.
(off Rte. 12A)
Cornish NH 03745
603-675-2175
Mid-May–October 31; daily 8:30-4:30.
Guided tours of the home, gardens and studios of Augustus Saint-Gaudens (1848-1907), one of America's foremost sculptors.
▶ I-89 to exit 20 or I-91 to exit 8 or 9, then to Rte 12A in Cornish.

Water Quality and the Connecticut River

"The objective of this act is to restore and maintain the chemical, physical, and biological integrity of the nation's waters."
    – Section 101(a) of the Federal Clean Water Act

Since passing the Clean Water Act in 1972, the Connecticut River has been substantially nursed back to health. Much of the organic material and bacteria that had been polluting the River has been removed. But according to Geoff Dates of the River Watch Network, "if we are to judge by the amounts of nutrient and toxic pollution in the River, many areas are no cleaner than they were, and some are more polluted."

The Clean Water Act set the national goal as the elimination of all pollution discharge into the navigable waters of the United States by 1985. That year has come and gone and still the River is threatened by pollution.

Non-point pollution – from urban landscapes and areas of disturbed earth such as logging sites and croplands – routinely dumps oil, grease, bacteria, nutrients, and soil sediment into the water. In addition, old sewage treatment plants must now either be overhauled or replaced, and new plants constructed. Finally, we must better understand the impact of toxic wastes on the environment and determine how to treat them.

According to Federal standards, Class A water is safe for drinking, Class B for swimming and fishing, and Class C primarily for industrial use. Depending on the time, most of the Connecticut River meets Class B standards. However, substantial stretches (e.g., a stretch near White River Junction, VT, as well as the Black River and Mill Brook) have been found with high bacteria, nutrient, and soil sediment levels after heavy rainfalls.

It seems we are willing to accept Class B water as clean, or at least as clean enough. Yet, one of the stated objectives of the Federal Clean Water Act is to maintain "the biological integrity of the nation's waters." This requires waters far cleaner than those considered Class B. In fact, waters which are clean enough for human use – and even for human drinking – are often too polluted to maintain the natural ecosystem.

If interest in the environment continues and increased funds are directed toward environmental clean-up, water quality in the Connecticut River will continue to improve. People who use the River and find it appealing must help keep it clean by removing trash, identifying polluters, and by working with local governments and businesses to stop pollution. Given time, many of the problems discussed above can be solved. However, if we continue to settle for waters that appear clean rather than working for a truly healthy River, the Clean Water Act will remain an elusive ideal rather than an achievable objective.

Fisheries of the River

The Connecticut River has the most diverse fish population of all the tributaries in New England. It includes native fish, fish that have been introduced, freshwater fish, saltwater visitors from Long Island Sound, and anadromous species that hatch in fresh water, mature in salt water, and return to fresh water to spawn.

In the northern stretches of the stream the River is dominated by trout: brown, rainbow, and brook. In the middle portion there is good fishing for cool-water species such as bass and walleye. In the lower reaches, anglers capitalize on largemouth bass, panfish, northern pike, catfish, eel, carp, white perch, and sometimes striped bass. The numerous coves and inlets along the lower River are often the most productive areas for many of the game-fishing species, although bait-fishing in the main channel during the summer rarely fails to produce good and varied catches.

In colonial days the Connecticut River was fabulously abundant with salmon, shad, sturgeon, and other anadromous fish. Salmon up to 30 pounds and more were reportedly taken in considerable numbers, and thousands of barrels of shad were put up for the Revolutionary army. Shad were so abundant that they were used as fertilizer, and indentured servants' contracts stipulated that they were not to be fed shad more than so many times a week. The salmon run was estimated at about 40,000 fish per year, and the shad run may have included as many as 7 million fish annually.

The building of dams on the River's tributaries in the early 1700s blocked off most of the salmon's spawning grounds. The construction of a dam across the River at Turner's Falls, MA, in 1798 eliminated the rest, causing the extermination of salmon and reducing the shad run considerably. Pollution–sewage and industrial waste–made the situation even more desperate.

The return of the Atlantic salmon has been slow. In 1870, the states of Maine, New Hampshire, Massachusetts, and Connecticut tried to reintroduce salmon to the River, but were unsuccessful because of technical and managerial problems. The effort was taken up again in 1967 with the passage of the Anadromous Fish Restoration Act, which provided federal aid for the project. In addition, fish ladders have been constructed by the power companies on all of the mainstream dams as far north as Wilder (or Hartford), VT. Currently, salmon entering the river at its mouth at Old Saybrook, CT, can migrate upstream over 212 miles, using five modern fishways, and enter the Ammonoosuc River in New Hampshire. As fishways are built around dams on this tributary, salmon will be able to ascend into the White Mountains. Great excitement was generated in 1985 when a salmon tagged and released at the Holyoke, MA fishway was sighted in a White River pool in central Vermont. It was the first salmon in the Green Mountains since George Washington's presidency. Fishways have also fully restored shad to its historic range in the river.

The salmon restoration project began with eggs from northern Canada. However, these eggs proved unsatisfactory because they were from an area too far north, and the fish had difficulty adapting to the Connecticut River, the southernmost river in which salmon spawned. After 11 years of trying with the eggs from Canada, all of 11 fish had returned. Eggs from the Penobscot River in Maine were then tried, with slightly better results: In the first year, 88 fish returned.

Initially, biologists had projected annual runs of 1,000 fish or more by 1986, and possibly a sport fishery by 1990. When the high returns didn't materialize, biologists conducted an in-depth review of the program, recognizing problems and shortcomings. Adjustments have been made in the program and a great deal of research has been initiated, aimed at providing answers to nagging questions. If climatic conditions in the North Atlantic cooperate, returning salmon are now expected to increase in 1991. Information gathered in the past five years indicates that restoration of salmon using a non-native strain is going to be more of a challenge than originally thought. Nevertheless, program biologists are still optimistic about the effort's long-term success. At this time, it is difficult to predict when the run will be large enough to warrant the opening of a sport fishery. Most returning adults continue to be trapped at the first fishway they encounter and are retained for breeding purposes. However, every tenth salmon trapped at the Holyoke fishway is tagged and released upstream. Therefore, boaters on the river may be passing over migrating sea-run salmon.

Because shad were never totally eradicated from the River, their return has been much speedier. The shad population is the second-largest in North America, and is expected to grow to the highest levels of the century during the 1990s.

Thousands of sport fishermen participate in the annual Shad Derby, and there are enough shad to support a commercial fishery. No longer regarded as something to be tossed into the ground as fertilizer, shad and shad roe are now considered a real delicacy. Many towns along the River have annual shad-bake festivals that attract large crowds. The art of removing the 1,500 bones of the shad is a closely held secret that is passed down from one generation to the next.

Determined and persistent efforts to abate pollution and clean up the Connecticut River have also played an important part in the development of better fishing. However, several municipalities along the River are still without sewage treatment plants, and a variety of industrial wastes continue to be dumped into the River.

Fishing licenses are required for all stretches of the River except south of the railroad bridge in Old Saybrook, CT–where saltwater fishing begins. Licenses are valid only in the states for which they are issued. Both resident and non-resident licenses permit fishing the River in Vermont and New Hampshire; these licenses are good in all waters between the two states and up to the first highway bridge spanning the tributaries which connect with the River. Regulations concerning seasons, fees, creel, and tackle limits may vary from state to state. For more information, we suggest you contact the appropriate state agency overseeing fishing in the River, listed in the Appendix.

Thanks to Stephen R. Gephard, Senior Fisheries Biologist with the Connecticut Department of Environmental Protection, for his help in compiling this article.

Birds of the Connecticut River Valley

The Connecticut River Valley provides a diverse range of habitats for resident species of birds, and considerable opportunities for migrating species to rest and feed on the way north or south. In the most northern reaches of the upper valley, spruce and fir forests provide breeding habitat for many Canadian zone species not found farther south. In the southern half of the upper valley and northern Massachusetts, the transitional Alleghenian zone predominates, with a mix of deciduous trees, white pine, and hemlock that provides habitat for a wide assortment of birds. With its broad floodplain, the lower Connecticut River Valley provides a distinctly different habitat for waterfowl, marsh and shore birds, and grass and farmland species. As the River moves toward and into Connecticut, the southern Carolinian zone begins to take over and a new set of species is found. Below Middletown, the River leaves the fertile valley and cuts through low eastern hills for 20 miles before reaching Long Island Sound. Here the coastal species dominate.

The Upper Valley

The Fourth Connecticut Lake is 2,500 feet above sea level, and although the River drops to 1,700 feet by the time it reaches First Lake, the surrounding mountains rise 3,000 to 5,000 feet. These high elevations are the home of the common loon, ringnecked duck, common goldeneye, and hooded and common merganser. In the forests are the bird-eating accipiter hawks and the little saw-whet owl. Great blue heron, American bittern, and snipe nest around the wetlands and beaver ponds. The fearless gray jay rules the campsites and picnic areas, and the raven's croak is heard on the cliff sides. The star of the coniferous forest is the warbler family: colorful little flyers, ever active in search of insects.

The Central Valley

The pool above the Turner's Falls Dam is one of the best sites for waterfowl in the spring. In the summer and early fall the daily rise and fall of the water level from the pumping project makes the pool an excellent spot for wading birds. The most bird-rich part of the valley in Massachusetts is probably the central basin from Deerfield to Northampton. There are large marshes adjoining the Deerfield River in Old Deerfield. Farther south, the Bradstreet Marshes in Hatfield are formed by an old oxbow of the River. In Northampton, the Arcadia Marshes and the east and west meadows provide low floodplain habitat.

The southern lowland is divided by the central ridge into a western area drained by the Westfield and Farmington rivers and an eastern area drained by the Connecticut River. There are extensive flood pools, fields, and marshes at the Stebbin Wildlife Refuge in Longmeadow, at Holyoke Cove in Agawam, and in South Windsor. Forest Park in Springfield is a favorite spot for migrant land birds. The exposed shoreline of the Connecticut River between Longmeadow and Agawam attracts a wide variety of birds during the summer and fall.

Arriving in the central valley as the water warms are both diving and dabbling ducks, as well as great blue herons and ospreys. The marshes in Deerfield, Hatfield, Northampton, Longmeadow, and South Windsor are good for sora, Virginia rail, and American bittern. The River and adjacent ponds also attract hordes of early swallows, particularly cliff swallows, and a few purple martins.

Westover, Barnes, and Turner's Falls airfields–as well as Bradley International Airport–have a limited population of upland sandpiper and grasshopper sparrow. A few horned larks and vesper sparrows reside in the intensively farmed areas of the floodplain. Kingfishers and bank swallows are regulars along the River and near other streams and ponds. Nighthawks buzz in the twilight over the urban centers.

Along the River from mid-July to mid-September great and snowy egrets and black-crowned night herons are regulars. Ring-billed gulls are abundant, and Bonaparte's gulls are fairly frequent. Common, black, and forester's terns have also been sighted.

Starting in September, the marshes in Deerfield, Hatfield, Northampton, Longmeadow, and South Windsor are gathering places for hundreds of dabbling ducks, many staying until late October or early November. Harvested or plowed fields attract golden plovers, yellowlegs, snipe, and pectoral sandpipers. Harriers begin to course the meadows, and an occasional merlin is spotted streaking across the sky. Water pipits may be found in the barrier fields, and tree and barn swallows congregate here for the flight south.

As the season progresses, the winter species begin to arrive: accipiters, rough-legged hawks, lapland longspurs, snow buntings, and, during flight years, flocks of redpolls. Herring gulls, great black-backed gulls, and ring-billed gulls feed at the landfills by the thousands and are joined by a few Iceland and glaucous gulls. Bald eagles are present on the River regularly in winter, but now a few can also be found year-round. Mallards, black ducks, and Canada geese will stay on late-freezing ponds or on the River if there is limited snow cover and food available nearby.

The Central Ridge

The central ridge in the lower valley ranges from 300 to 900 feet high and appears to be a trap or corridor for birds. The Mt. Tom Reservation in Holyoke and Easthampton is the largest accessible area for birding.

Hawks are the most famous specialty there. The large fall flights are traditionally observed from Goat's Peak, as well as from Skinner State Park on Mt. Holyoke in Hadley. Most migrants do not follow the ridges, but rather use the updrafts on the west and north side, coming in close for easy viewing. The most common migrant is the broad-winged hawk, of which hundreds or thousands can be seen in a single day. There is also a number of sharp-shinned hawks, ospreys, red-tailed hawks, and American kestrels. Migrating snow geese and double-crested cormorants are also regularly seen from the lookouts.

The best places to visit besides Mt. Tom are the various reservoirs and parks in West Hartford, Robinson State Park in Agawam, and Ashley ponds in Holyoke. The extensive spruce plantings at these locations are good sites in winter for finches as well as the boreal chickadee, red-breasted nuthatch, golden-crowned kinglet, and pine siskin.

The Tidal River

All the water birds and southern species already discussed become common at the mouth of the River. The marshes and estuaries of Old Saybrook and Old Lyme are a stronghold for the double-crested cormorant, great blue heron, great and snowy egret, black-crowned night heron, and glossy ibis. Mute swans, Canada geese, and several duck species are also abundant. During winter and migration, other common waterfowl include the gadwall, pintail, teal, American wigeon, ring-necked duck, canvasback, scaup, common goldeneye, bufflehead, old-squaw, common eider, scoter, and merganser.

Ospreys and a few northern harriers nest along the shore. During fall migration, hundreds of American kestrels, sharp-shinned hawks and cooper's hawks, and a few merlins and peregrine falcons migrate past Griswold Point on Long Island Sound. In winter, Essex and Haddam Neck are favorite spots for bald eagles, who sit in the trees on the lookout for fish and waterfowl. As elsewhere, the shoreline population of eagles and ospreys has increased dramatically since the banning of DDT.

Rails hide in the marshes, and migrating plovers and sandpipers gather by the thousands in May and July through September to feed on the mud flats at low tide or rest in the salt marshes when the water is high. Herring gulls and great black-backed gulls are always present. In summer, common and least terns fish and nest along the inlets and beaches. Fish crows are also likely to be found there. Marsh wrens are in the cattails, and there are two species of sparrow that are found only in the sedge marshes: the sharp-tailed and the seaside sparrow.

Camping on the River

There are many people who boat, fish, canoe, and swim in the Connecticut River. An effort by each individual to be responsible for his or her own activities will result in a significant contribution to keeping the Connecticut River clean and enjoyable. The River's ecosystem is fragile and relies upon your care for its survival.

It is important to realize that most of the shoreline and islands of the River are privately owned. Under no circumstances should anyone use private property to camp, picnic, or obtain access without *first* getting permission of the owner. Be pleasant. Good manners will help open the way. Remember that if you do not obtain permission, you are liable for charges of trespassing and vandalism. In general, landowners will grant permission if they are assured that you will take care of their property.

Always leave your campsite immaculate. That way, the next time you or someone else requests permission to camp there will not be a problem. Only public landings and established campsites are mentioned in this book, although there are many areas that are suitable for camping if permission is obtained from the owner. Always contact park managers to make advance reservations in order to avoid unhappy surprises during your trip. Here are a few guidelines to follow when camping on the river:

1. You *must* carry out what you carry in. Not only does common sense dictate that you leave the site clean for the next person, but littering is also prohibited by law.

2. Use public bathroom facilities at established campgrounds or shoreline communities whenever possible. In remote areas, bury personal waste at least 100 feet from the River's edge.

3. Use portable stoves instead of building fires (which are illegal in some areas). This leaves the ground cover undisturbed and reduces the risk of forest fires.

4. Always use biodegradable soaps.

5. Since most of the River and tributaries are not potable, always be sure to take along plenty of drinking water.

6. Do not cut vegetation or dig holes along the shore or engage in other activities that might cause bank erosion.

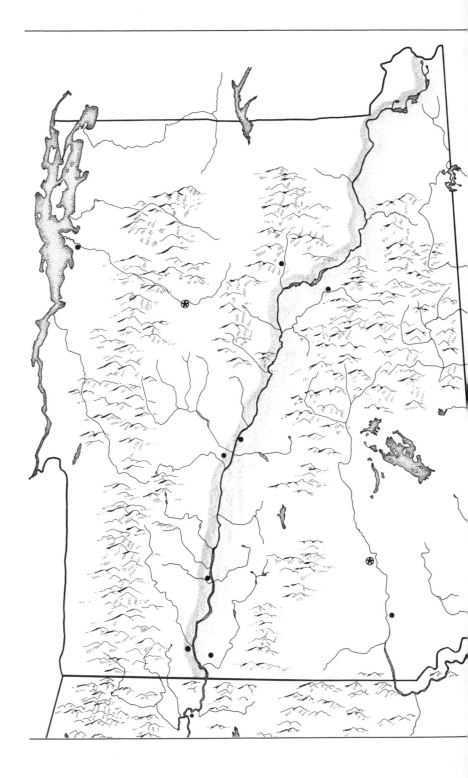

New Hampshire
and Vermont

© *Connecticut River Watershed Council/Nacul Center*

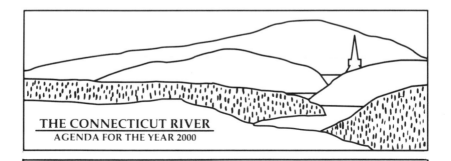

THE CONNECTICUT RIVER
AGENDA FOR THE YEAR 2000

Help Us Create a Greenway

Connecticut River Valley Resource Commission, NH
Connecticut River Watershed Advisory Commission, VT

P.O. Box 1182
Charlestown, NH 03603

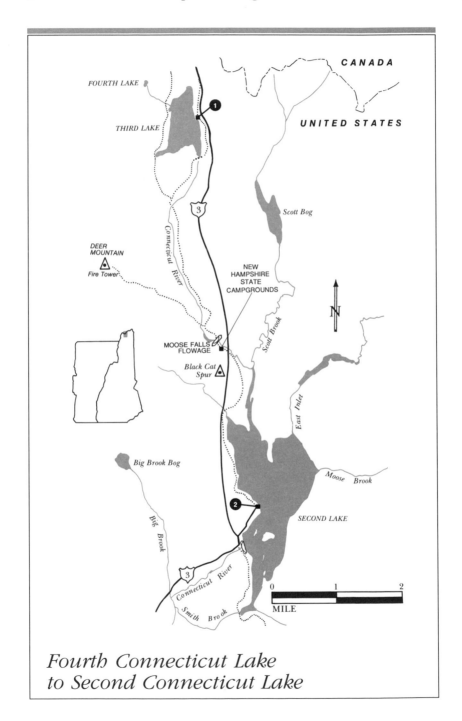

Fourth Connecticut Lake
to Second Connecticut Lake

Fourth Connecticut Lake
to Second Connecticut Lake

MILE FROM MOUTH:	410-400 (10.0 mile span).
NAVIGABLE BY:	Kayak, canoe, small powerboats and sailboats on the lakes only.
PORTAGES:	Mile 410, Fourth Lake to Third Lake, 1/2 mile. Mile 408.5, Third Lake to Second Lake, 4 miles. Mile 400, Second Lake to First Lake, 2 miles.
CAMPING:	Deer Mountain Campground, Pittsburg, NH (no telephone).
USGS MAPS:	Second Connecticut Lake 15.
EMERGENCY HELP:	Pittsburg, NH (603) 538-7003. Colebrook, NH (603) 237-5555, CB 19.

The Connecticut River begins in the clouds above the mountains of Canada and New Hampshire. Falling rain collects and creates tiny rivulets that join together in a hollow among the spruce and fir trees, thus giving shape to the Fourth Connecticut Lake just 300 yards south of the U.S./Canada border. Modest as it is, this little lake is the source of the majestic and historic Connecticut River which flows 410 miles, through four states, and eventually empties into the Atlantic Ocean at Long Island Sound.

To reach the **Fourth Connecticut Lake,** which is worth the effort, you must go by foot. Begin at the U.S. Customs House on Rte. 3 at the Quebec/New Hampshire border. The trail is frequently muddy so watch your step and dress appropriately. (It is probably best to notify the customs officer that you plan to hike to the Fourth Connecticut Lake, as a safety precaution.) You will see a sign outside the customs house marking the beginning of the approximately 3/4 mile trail which has been recently cleared, so you should have little trouble finding your way. The lake is about 120 yards long and quite wild. Keep a lookout for wildlife: beaver, red-tailed hawks, otters, mergansers, ducks, loons, deer, black bear, moose – they're all here. Fortunately, the land surrounding Fourth Lake has recently been donated to the Nature Conservancy, so we all will be able to enjoy the wilds of the Fourth Lake for years to come.

If you're intrigued with conundrums and have some time, go about one mile across the Canadian border to **Magnetic Hill** in Quebec. The

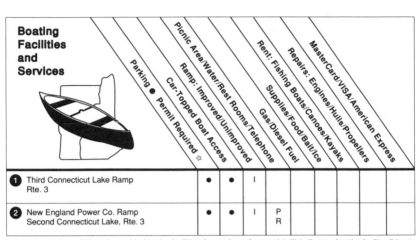

Boating Facilities and Services	Parking ● Permit Required ☆	Car-Topped Boat Access	Ramp: Improved/Unimproved	Picnic Area/Water/Rest Rooms/Telephone	Gas/Diesel Fuel	Supplies/Food/Bait/Ice	Rent: Fishing Boats/Canoes/Kayaks	Repairs: Engines/Hulls/Propellers	MasterCard/VISA/American Express
① Third Connecticut Lake Ramp Rte. 3	●	●	I						
② New England Power Co. Ramp Second Connecticut Lake, Rte. 3	●	●	I	P R					

Information in these listings is provided by the facilities themselves. An asterisk (*) indicates that the facility did not respond to our most recent requests for information.

panoramic view and picnic area at the top of the hill are reward enough, but there is more to this area than just beauty. Drive your automobile to the bottom of the hill and stop. Put the transmission in neutral and watch as you begin to roll *uphill.* Not convinced? Look at the water in the stream next to the road; it, too, is flowing uphill. The gravitational pull of the moon perhaps? A quirk of science? You figure it out.

Between Fourth and Third Lakes, the River is shallow, congested with trees, bushes, beaver dams, and great for trout fishing. But, due to its small size, it is not suited to navigation. Here, you can say without exaggeration, that you leapt across the Connecticut River in a single bound.

The **Third Connecticut Lake,** with its crystalline waters nestled at the base of wooded hills, is a good place for birding, trout fishing, canoeing, or just walking along the shore. The lake reaches a maximum depth of about 100 feet and is accessible by a boat ramp right off Rte. 3. At the southeastern end of the lake, the River exits amid fallen trees, a number of beaver dams and lodges, and is once again mostly unnavigable although, under certain flow conditions, expert kayakers have attempted it. If you're not an expert kayaker, stick to the road.

Following Rte. 3 down from the Third Connecticut Lake to the Second Lake you will note a small white cross on the side of the road. This cross, which is maintained by the state of New Hampshire Highway Department, marks the site where on May 10, 1940 an unidentifed man was found dead, a victim of exposure. The man entered the U.S. from Canada under an alias on February 22, 1940. Since at this time there was no open highway, traveling was a serious endeavor and unfortunately this fellow never made it to his destination.

Continuing south, **Moose Falls Flowage** appears along Rte. 3 immediately before the **Deer Mountain Campground** where the Connecticut River crosses under the highway. The Flowage, which is a small lakelike area full of submerged stumps and beaver lodges, was created by Moose Falls Dam and is a good place to paddle around in a canoe or do some birding. The Deer Mountain Campground, which is run by the state of New Hampshire, boasts of fresh spring water and has tent sites right along the River affording a wonderous view of **Deer Mountain** – a great 3-4 hour climb for the serious hiker.

When driving on Rte. 3, notice the low, wet, boglike areas along the road. These are moose wallows. If you're interested in seeing some moose, wallows are the place to look – usually at early morning and dusk. Note, however, that at times the moose are on the road and usually not in too great a hurry to move. Drive accordingly.

The **Second Connecticut Lake,** which is approximately 4 miles in length, is accessible by a New England Power Company boat launch on the western shore. The launch has plenty of parking, a concrete ramp, and a picnic area. North of the lake, **Scott Bog** and **East Inlet** are quiet havens for canoeing, fishing, and moose sightings. Both spots are accessible by East Inlet Road, which is a gravel road veering east off of Rte. 3 just south of Deer Mountain Campground. While on the Second Lake, if you're using a canoe, keep in mind that this is a big stretch of water which can produce sizable waves. There is a general consensus among canoeing authorities that there is no sense in swamping a canoe if it can be avoided. Be prudent, especially here. There aren't too many people living in this region so help may be hard to come by.

At the southwestern corner of the Second Lake, just below two heavily wooded islands, is the Second Connecticut Lake Dam, owned and operated by the New England Power Company. It is an impressive sight and certainly worth some investigation. Flowage information about the dam is available from the New England Power at (603) 448-2200.

© Connecticut River Watershed Council

Dr. and Mrs. Davidson at the Connecticut Lakes.

SOURCE TO THE SEA:
A TRIP DOWN THE CONNECTICUT RIVER

The Connecticut River has been a highway through the lands of central New England since the earliest times. There is no record, however, of anyone traveling from the highest source of the Connecticut River – Fourth Connecticut Lake – to Long Island until the trip was undertaken in 1959 by a group led by the president of The Connecticut River Watershed Council, Dr. Joseph G.Davidson. The Davidsons made the trip in seven days by canoe, powerboat, and car to "preach the gospel of conversation at every stop."

On the first day of the journey their party hiked into Fourth Connecticut Lake where Dr. Davidson filled "a jug of clear sparkling water, the kind which leaves the source of the Connecticut in its long voyage to the sea." They all had a drink of the water and Dr. Davidson noted sadly that this was "the last drink we'll take from the Connecticut." From Camp Idlewild on Second Connecticut Lake the party drove to Groveton, NH, then paddled by canoe to Guildhall, VT, where they were greeted by Vermont Governor Robert T. Stafford. From there they continued by boat and automobile to Hanover, NH, and the Wilder Dam.

From Wilder, riding in a turbojet-propelled boat, Dr. Davidson and his wife were taken down through the Hartland Rapids (Sumner Falls), where they came to grief. The boat hit a submerged rock. The travelers, however, were unhurt and transferred to other transportation for the trip to Charlestown, NH. Dr. Davidson was later reminded by a friend that these same rapids gave Major Rogers and his Rogers Rangers serious troubles on their journey from St. Francis, Quebec, to Fort No. 4 at Charlestown.

The Davidsons continued their trip, visiting schools, flood-control projects, pollution-control projects, and recreational sites along the River. In Bellows Falls, VT, they were greeted by a band and a parade and were treated to a steamboat ride to Brattleboro, VT.

Continuing into Massachusetts, they visited the fish lift at Holyoke Dam that had assisted 15,000 shad upriver the previous year. The Davidsons completed the trip from West Springfield, MA, to Long Island Sound in a day. They viewed bank erosion, the historic Windsor Locks, and met with Connecticut Lieutenant Governor John Dempsey and other state officials on this final, eventful day.

At the end of the trip, Dr. Davidson displayed the two jugs of water he had collected at the Fourth Connecticut Lake and another – obviously polluted – jugful collected from farther downstream. He spoke of the River as being a treasure that had become an open sewage and recalled donning a gas mask at several beautiful but odiferous locations on the trip downstream.

Dr. Davidson's mission was to raise the consciousness of the public and of the responsible officials to both the beauty of and the damage to the Connecticut River. In this he was successful.   ✦

© Clyde Smith

The Fourth Connecticut Lake.

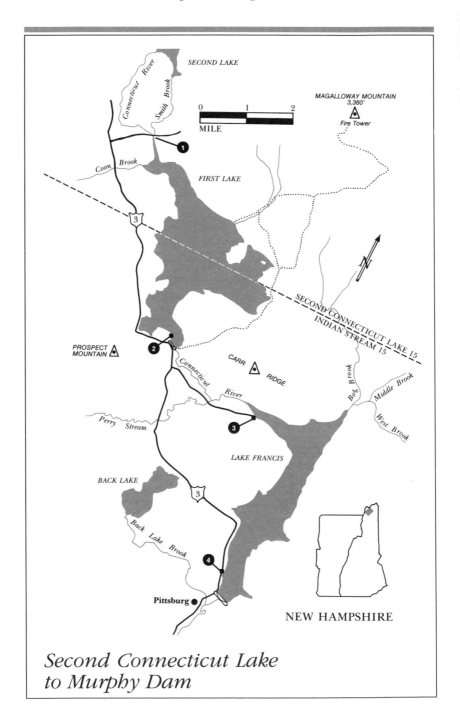

SECOND LAKE

Connecticut River

Smith Brook

MAGALLOWAY MOUNTAIN
3,360'
Fire Tower

0   1   2
MILE

❶

Coon Brook

FIRST LAKE

N

3

SECOND CONNECTICUT LAKE 15

INDIAN STREAM 15

PROSPECT
MOUNTAIN

❷

Connecticut

River

CARR   RIDGE

Bog Brook

Middle Brook

Perry Stream

❸

West Brook

LAKE FRANCIS

BACK LAKE

3

Back Lake Brook

❹

Pittsburg ●

NEW HAMPSHIRE

*Second Connecticut Lake
to Murphy Dam*

Second Connecticut Lake to Murphy Dam

MILE FROM MOUTH:	400 to 383 (17 mile span).
NAVIGABLE BY:	Kayak, canoe; small powerboats and sailboats on the lakes.
DIFFICULTY:	Class II-VI, depending on flow conditions; flat water on the lakes.
PORTAGES:	Mile 400, Second Lake to First Lake, 2 miles. Mile 395, First Lake to Lake Francis, 2 miles.
CAMPING:	Mile 387.5, Lake Francis State Park, Pittsburg, NH (603) 538-6965.
USGS MAPS:	Second Connecticut Lake 15. Indian Stream 15.
EMERGENCY HELP:	Pittsburg, NH (603) 538-7033. Colebrook, NH (603) 237-5555, CB 19.

The Connecticut River begins as a trickle leading into the Fourth Connecticut Lake and builds volume over the ten mile stretch leading to the bottom of the Second Lake. Water surges south from rivulets running along the border between Canada and the United States, a winding stretch known as "the height of the land." Then in the three short miles from the Second Lake to the First, the River again gathers force before beginning a rapid descent of nearly 200 feet, scratching its way along a narrow bed of granite. Forced through this constriction, the water rises in rapids that will challenge even the most experienced paddler.

DANGER: *The 3-mile span between Second Lake and First Lake, which quickly drops 200 feet, should be run by experts only, and then only in covered boats after meticulous scouting from land. Even so, anyone who chooses to challenge this section will have to portage his/her boat around several waterfalls. As there are no cut trails, bushwhacking will be in order. Smith Brook parallels the path of the River, but without the same volume. The brook can be explored by expert boaters only, and then in the best conditions – when the water is high.*

Boating Facilities and Services	Parking ● Permit Required ☆	Car-Topped Boat Access	Ramp: Improved/Unimproved	Picnic Area/Water/Rest Rooms/Telephone	Gas/Diesel Fuel	Supplies/Food/Bait/Ice	Rent: Fishing Boats/Canoes/Kayaks	Repairs: Engines/Hulls/Propellers	MasterCard/VISA/American Express
1 Magalloway Road Bridge Magalloway Road		●							
2 New England Power Co. First Lake Ramp Rte. 3	●	●	I	P R					
3 Lake Francis State Park River Road (603) 538-6965	●	●	I	PR W					
4 Lake Francis Ramp Rte. 3	●	●	I						

Information in these listings is provided by the facilities themselves. An asterisk (*) indicates that the facility did not respond to our most recent requests for information.

Below the rapids, **First Lake** broadens into a serene and calm beauty that belies the rocky descent above. The lake may be easily explored in canoes, kayaks, runabouts, or even small sailboats. There is plenty of room to maneuver among the fishing boats and more than a few coves and small islands to explore on a lazy afternoon. The town of **Pittsburg** has a long-standing ordinance against overnight camping or fires, so don't try to establish either unless you know you're on land set aside for that purpose; and do not camp on New England Power Company land,which is also off-limits to overnight visits.

Trailered boats should put in at the **NEP ramp** above the dam. Next to the ramp is a recreation area replete with picnic tables, grills, beaches, and toilets. Car-topped boats may be put in here or at the **Magalloway Road** bridge marking First Lake's northernmost tip. Above the bridge, fishing is not allowed; below it there is a limit of 2 catches per day.

If you are spending a day or two in the Pittsburg area, you will want to hike up **Magalloway Mountain,** whose peak is about 8 miles from Rte. 3. (You may drive to the base of the mountain and then hike about a mile to the fire tower.) From the fire tower, you can see each of the Connecticut Lakes and much of the surrounding countryside. First Lake is about five miles long, and if you could peer through the water, you would see the original border of the lake before the dam was built. Many trees were cut along the banks before the lake was allowed to expand over its natural shoreline, and today many of those trunks poke up along the shore. First Lake is much deeper than its counterparts and attracts many fishermen. Coupled with a stiff breeze, the long fetch on First Lake often creates a serious chop, with whitecaps that will rock even powerboats. Be sure to wear a lifejacket at all times. Coming from the Magalloway Bridge, the water is flat and serene. You will pass fishermen in waders and small boats. As you enter the Lake itself, the rocky shores are beautifully wooded with fir and spruce trees, reminiscent of Maine's weathered landscape. Most of the land along the water, including the grey rocks and the driftwood cut by local beavers, is owned by the power company. The forests themselves are owned by Champion International Corp., which uses the timber for lumber and paper products.

Heading out to the large peninsula on the northern shore can be a struggle, especially if the wind is up. On the western side of the peninsula there is a notch in the granite shore that most boats can sidle into. Tie a line to the trees and scramble up the rocks to a small, wooden shelter and then fight off the urge to stay here overnight – there is a fireplace and an outhouse but camping is not allowed.

The water in First Lake is controlled by a **New England Power Company dam** at the south end. You can find the daily water-release schedules in the local Colebrook paper or by calling New England Power Company (603) 448-2200. You may also write to NEP at P.O. Box 528, Lebanon, NH 03766.

DANGER: All boaters must beware of the water-release schedules at the Connecticut Lake dams. This is especially important when running the River between First Lake and Lake Francis. This stretch of River, which is roughly 3 miles long, should be attempted only by experts in covered boats, and then only when water is not being released.

The first mile of River below the dam is steep and bumpy, followed by a mile of easy rapids. Once **Perry Stream** enters from the west, however, the going gets rough. With the influx of new water and a long drop to **Lake Francis,** the last 3/4 of a mile will challenge even the finest whitewater paddlers. If the water is high, you may want to portage until you reach the Lake. At any rate, be sure to scout the area before proceeding.

Lake Francis is the only manmade lake in the Connecticut chain. In 1940 the State of New Hampshire built a 100-foot-high dam just north of Pittsburg, and now the lake is a favorite among boaters and fishermen. (Incidentally, the town of Pittsburg, which encompasses some 300 square miles, is the largest township east of the Mississippi, a full 1/3 the size of Rhode Island.) Like First Lake, Lake Francis is about 5 miles long. Running almost due north, the wind whips along the length of the lake as though it has been forced through a funnel, often causing whitecaps to arise.

Lake Francis covers what used to be one of the twistiest sections of the upper River. When the dam was built, however, many square miles of land were permanently flooded. If you have the chance to look at an old topographical map, you'll see exactly how much woodland was lost.

You may want to begin your trip along Lake Francis at **Lake Francis State Park,** on the west bank near where the River empties into the lake. The large, well-kept park is easily accessible from Rte. 3, where you'll find many signs directing you. There are a number of campsites with fireplaces, tables, and trash barrels; and for those wishing to camp with the luxuries of home, there is a nice bathroom with showers. The gravel boat ramp is wide and can handle almost all trailered boats.

Heading toward the lake's northernmost point, where **Bog, Middle,** and **West Brooks** merge into the **Cedar Stream** rapids, you'll be in open water passing along a sloping shore. Most of the land around the lake is owned by the State of New Hampshire Water Resource Council, a quasi-governmental organization formed to protect the land. In a few places, however, cabins and houses dot the shoreline. Reaching the confluence of the brooks, the water has a faintly brown color; this comes from the tannic acid released by the needles and bark of the spruce and cedar trees in the area. Tannic acid is renowned for its healing qualities, so you may want to splash water on the scrapes you've picked up along the way.

On the southwest shore above the dam is a small, paved ramp. Neither camping nor open fires are allowed here, but this is a good place to remove your boat after having begun a trip at the State Park or even farther north. You may continue down to the dam, but there is no car access nearby. Portages should begin at the ramp, though if you don't mind climbing up and down with boat in hand, you can pull out a canoe or kayak in the little cove on the west shore above the dam. From there, you should be able to sneak down and around the water flow. Finding a place to put in below the dam requires a willingness to bushwhack and get your feet wet, as well as serendipity. 🌲

ACID PRECIPITATION

The true source of the Connecticut River is not the lakes, streams, and bogs of New England but the clouds. Rain and snow fall across the land and trickle through the soil, forming the countless tributaries that drain into the Connecticut.

The precipitation that falls today hardly resembles that which has fed the River historically. Today, the rain and the snow are poisoned with acids from industrial pollution and automobile traffic. Sulphur emissions from factories become sulphuric acid when combined with water, just as nitrous oxide becomes nitric acid. Burning coal to produce electricity produces sulphur, while cars and trucks produce nitrous oxide. The transformation of these emissions into acid occurs in the atmosphere and is then transported back to earth in rainwater.

In some areas of the world, the soil can neutralize these acids. In the mountains and rocky landscapes of New England, however, the soil is not rich enough to buffer these poisons. And when the precipitation becomes so acidic that the soil can no longer neutralize the water, aluminum in the bedrock is released into the watertable. Generally, this aluminum proves toxic to fish and other species in the food chain. Today, the many lakes and streams are so acidic that they can no longer maintain fish or other life.

Forests are also affected by acid rain. Scientists have linked dieback at high elevations to the acid rain, and there is evidence that the decrease in productivity associated with the sugar maple is also due to acid rain. The problems that acid precipitation creates are not isolated to any one region or nation – they affect the entire planet. Unfortunately, the international scope of both pollution creation and acid rain make this a particularly difficult problem to solve. The on-going destruction of Canadian freshwater from pollutants created in the United States has forced those nations to work together in search of a solution. Hopefully, that example will induce other nations to sit down together in an effort to stop the pollution that is quickly destroying the freshwater on the earth. ✦

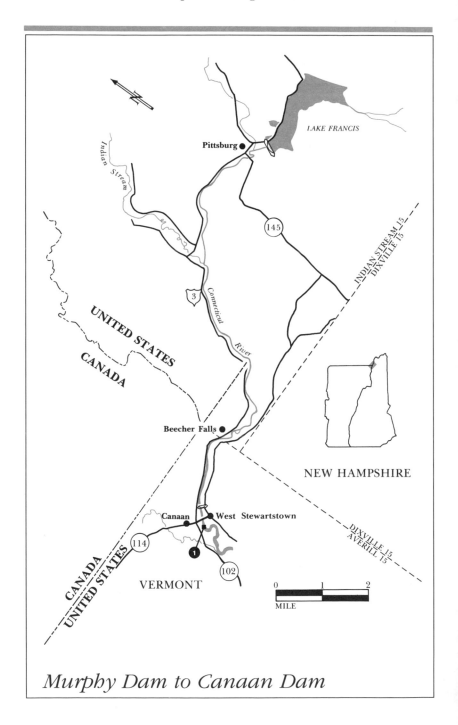

Murphy Dam to Canaan Dam

Murphy Dam to Canaan Dam

MILE FROM MOUTH:	383-373 (10 mile span).
NAVIGABLE BY:	Kayak, canoe.
DIFFICULTY:	Class I-III.
PORTAGES:	Mile 373, Canaan Dam, west side, 1/2 mile.
CAMPING:	No established sites.
USGS MAPS:	Indian Stream 15. Averill 15.
EMERGENCY HELP:	Pittsburg, NH (603) 538-7003. Canaan, VT (802) 266-3400. Colebrook, NH (603) 237-5555, CB 19.

The water running below Murphy Dam on Lake Francis varies greatly depending on the season. In spring, when the River is full from the early freshet, you may be able to canoe the four-mile stretch from the covered bridge, below the dam, to Indian Stream; otherwise, it's best to put in at Indian Stream and work down from there, where the water is higher. The falls at the covered bridge are spectacular and should be seen by all.

The stretch of River from **Indian Stream** to **Beecher Falls** is easily managed by everyone except the most inexperienced canoeists. There are a few rapids now and again, adding a bit of spice to the trip, but generally the greatest challenge will be keeping the boat heading straight and moving forward. During summer when the water is low, paddling can prove a bit scratchy until you reach Beecher Falls; then the River receives another surge of water, this time from **Hall Stream,** which flows south along the border between the United States and Canada.

It's easy to mistake the turn into Hall Stream for the continuance of the Connecticut River, which runs to the west. You'll soon know of your mistake, however, as you will face an increasingly stiff current. After passing beneath the cement **Rte. 3 bridge,** Hall Stream runs along a short residential area before leading you to a large lumber mill. From here the stream starts to get shallow and continuing up can be a struggle.

Hall Stream and Indian Stream run roughly parallel and are about four miles apart. During the early 1800s, the low area between these two

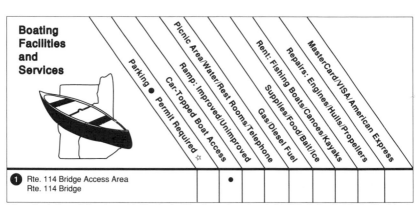

	Parking ● Permit Required ☆	Car-Topped Boat Access	Ramp: Improved/Unimproved	Picnic Area/Water/Rest Rooms/Telephone	Gas/Diesel Fuel	Supplies/Food/Bait/Ice	Rent: Fishing Boats/Canoes/Kayaks	Repairs: Engines/Hulls/Propellers	MasterCard/VISA/American Express
1 Rte. 114 Bridge Access Area Rte. 114 Bridge				●					

Information in these listings is provided by the facilities themselves. An asterisk (*) indicates that the facility did not respond to our most recent requests for information.

streams was the site of a farming community called the **Indian Stream Republic.** The land must have looked much then as it does today, without the rocky soil that you'll see farther south in New Hampshire. As farmers came to till this land, they were perched in a no-man's land between Canada and the United States. On Rte. 3 in Pittsburg, there is a marker telling the story of how the village declared itself an independent state with no allegiance to either nation, which led to a series of skirmishes known as the Indian Stream War.

Continuing down the Connecticut River, you will head over **Beecher Falls.** The River here is usually Class II, but after a heavy rain or after water has been released from Murphy Dam, the rapids increase in difficulty to Class III. At these times, beginners may want to portage around the falls. If you choose to test your skills and head through the falls, be sure to keep the canoe heading straight through the rapids and try to stay in the slower water nearer the banks. Whatever your passage, you should scout the waters first from land. Fast water continues from Beecher Falls south.

Ethan Allen, Inc. began making furniture in Beecher Falls in 1936. The original factory (802) 266-3355, which is now one of 25 across the nation, continues to make living room and bedroom furniture. Tours of the factory are given Monday through Thursday at 10 a.m. and 1 p.m. Visitors can watch a film on furniture making and see the finish room where stains and varnishes are applied before the furniture is packaged for shipment.

Continuing past **Canaan Dam** requires portaging. You can take your boat out on the Vermont shore just above the dam. From there, follow the paved road which leads to the **Rte. 114 bridge** where you will see an access point just below the bridge. The entire portage is about 1/2 mile long. Below the dam the current runs quickly. Be sure to keep a tight hold on your canoe before you've settled in or it might get away. 🌲

© *Clyde Smith*

© *Connecticut River Watershed Council/Nacul Center*

THE GLORIOUS SAGA
OF INDIAN STREAM

At the close of the American Revolution, the Treaty of Paris set the Canadian-United States boundary – imperfectly, it seems. Running westward between the St. Lawrence River Basin and the many streams wending south toward New Hampshire, the border was to touch the imprecise point at the northwesternmost head of the Connecticut River.

It was there, around 1824, that a roughshod community of farmers and backwoodsmen formed a settlement called Indian Stream. Not exactly part of the United States or Canada, the village seemed perched in an odd limbo; and though many settlers came to work the fertile bottomland, others followed hoping to escape the law.

Except when it came time to collect taxes and conscript men for service, Indian Stream suffered the indifferences of both the United States and Canada. The people of the town soon grew tired of this situation, and, determined not to ally themselves with either nation, they established their own country – the Indian Stream Republic.

With a constitution and a bicameral Congress, the Republic began improving the school system and cleaning up the riff-raff, who were often imprisoned on a flat rock beneath a large overturned kettle. But the little nation was still ignored by its two neighbors – except when the United States came to take soldiers. Things finally came to a head when a sheriff from New Hampshire came to arrest a local man named John Tyler.

The sheriff foolishly enlisted the help of another Indian Streamer named Richard Blanchard, and the two men took Tyler prisoner. After holding him for a few hours, Tyler's friends came to his rescue, leaving behind an embarrassed sheriff wondering how he could retrieve his prisoner, who had fled to Canada.

In a thoughtful stroke of tit-for-tat, Tyler sneaked back into Indian Stream and kidnapped Blanchard, who was taken to Canada for safe keeping. Blanchard had friends of his own, however, and they took little time invading Canada to set him free. This was the first of two northern invasions that occurred in the next two weeks, to be known thenceforth as the Indian Stream War.

With Blanchard safely returned home and Tyler resting peaceably across the border, it seemed the game had come to a close – until the sheriff from New Hampshire mucked things up again, that is.

Soothing his wounded pride over grog at the local tavern, the sheriff was determined not to be outdone. To rectify his loss, he offered a five dollar reward for the re-capture of John Tyler, and the chase was on.

In the 1820s, way up north in the hinterlands, $5 was a virtual fortune, and the promise of earning it honestly sent a crowd of intoxicated men stumbling through the woods toward Canada that evening. Upon crossing the border, they were surprised to find a large group of Canadians gathered to meet them. Loud voices soon led to a struggle, and two men – Ephraim Aldrich of Indian Stream and Justice Rea of Canada – broke from the crowd and set off down a wooded road, Aldrich chasing Rea with a sword.

After tripping Rea from behind, Aldrich attempted to stab his opponent in the chest. Fortunately, he missed and the point stuck in the mud. With Rea holding the blade tightly, the struggle fizzled into a temper tantrum.

> "Let go of my sword," Aldrich yelled.
> "I will if you leave me alone," Rea said.
> "I'll leave you alone, if you let go of my sword."
> "Well, it's stuck in the mud."

And so on and so forth until the crowd arrived and split the men up. Rea was carried away to have his hands bandaged, and Aldrich extricated his sword before wandering off to find his horse. John Tyler remained at large, and the sheriff returned home humiliated with $5 still in his pocket.

Though New Hampshire sent in a few troops to maintain the peace, the Indian Stream Republic finally received the attention it needed. The boundary dispute was settled, and though many people opposed it, the Republic was quietly absorbed into Coos County, NH, where it remains today. The town has since been renamed Pittsburg, but the place remains much the same. Many of the residents are descended from the crew that started the Republic, and though cars now travel the streets instead of horses, the promise of $5 can still raise quite a fuss. ✦

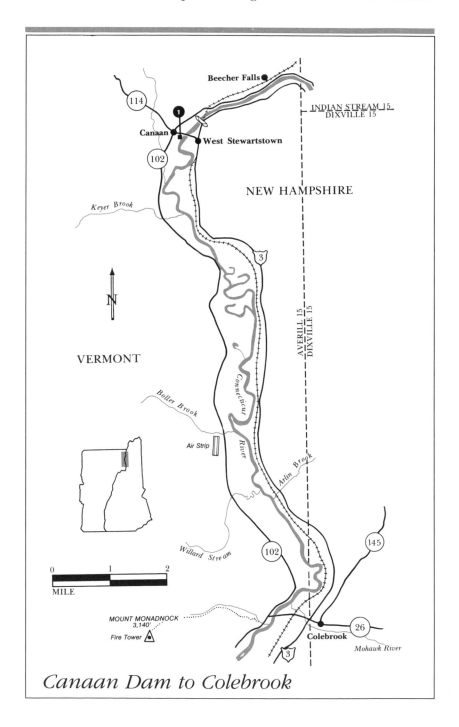

Canaan Dam to Colebrook

Canaan Dam to Colebrook

MILE FROM MOUTH:	373-363 (10 mile span).
NAVIGABLE BY:	Kayak, canoe.
DIFFICULTY:	Class I-II.
PORTAGES:	None.
CAMPING:	No established sites.
USGS MAPS:	Averill 15. Dixville 15.
EMERGENCY HELP:	Canaan, VT (802) 266-3400. Colebrook, NH (603) 237-5555, CB 19.

A quick look at the map will reveal the character of the River between Canaan and Colebrook: gentle and meandering. Through pastures and barnyards, beneath the mighty Mount Monadnock, and with Vermont to the west and New Hampshire to the east, the Connecticut River slowly winds southward carving out steep, muddy banks and oxbows in the rural New England landscape. This stretch of river will be most enjoyable for those interested in a pleasant afternoon of smooth canoeing.

Immediately below the **Rte. 114 bridge** on the Canaan side is a dirt road leading down to an access point on the River. This is an unimproved access point, however, with a wooden embankment and some hefty rocks – be prepared to do some maneuvering with your canoe or kayak. As you make your way down the River, you'll notice many red-winged blackbirds wisping about, as well as yellow warblers and swallows. While the blackbirds, with their brightly colored wing patches, are quite beautiful, the warblers and swallows will most likely capture your attention as they shoot across the water's surface, darting from left to right, seeming to defy gravity and inertia.

In the distance, wooded hills, thick with birch, spruce, fir, and pine, rise on the horizon. During the 19th century much of this area was logged for pulpwood and lumber. Great rafts of timber were floated down the River to mills as far south as Holyoke, MA. Nearer the River's shore, sloping fields and pastures of the area farms lie atop the land. You may see a few cows or sheep; an abandoned tractor or two; and at particular

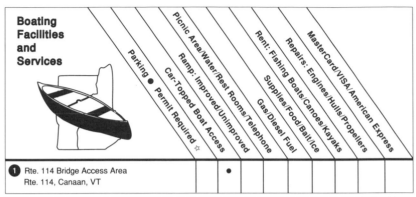

Boating Facilities and Services	Parking ●	Permit Required ☆	Car-Topped Boat Access	Ramp: Improved/Unimproved	Picnic Area/Water/Rest Rooms/Telephone	Rent: Fishing Boats/Canoes/Kayaks	Supplies/Food/Bait/Ice	Gas/Diesel Fuel	Repairs: Engines/Hulls/Propellers	MasterCard/VISA/American Express
1 Rte. 114 Bridge Access Area Rte. 114, Canaan, VT			●							

Information in these listings is provided by the facilities themselves. An asterisk (*) indicates that the facility did not respond to our most recent requests for information.

© *Embassy*

Access Area below Rte. 114 in Canaan, VT.

and not infrequent points along the way you will notice that certain scent which tends to accompany barnyards. Be forewarned.

Generally, the water is Class I, although during July and August the River can get low, thus making for more difficult paddling. Also, near Vermont's Mount Monadnock, strong winds are occasionally channeled down the valley creating a headwind.

Where **Arlin Brook** comes in from the New Hampshire side at mile 369.5 it is possible to get fresh water from the rest stop on Rte 3. Just above the **Colebrook Bridge,** Rte. 26 [373], there is a small, informal canoe access site. You can walk across to the Vermont side and reach the 2.4 mile trail up **Mt. Monadnock.** The view from atop Mt. Monadnock of the surrounding valley is spectacular. It is a solid hike, so plan on 3 hours for the round trip. You will notice, about 1/3 the way up, a picturesque waterfall that makes a good snacking spot. 🔳

NATURAL-VALLEY FLOOD STORAGE

The broad, flat 12,000-acre floodplain that stretches from West Stewartstown to Lancaster, NH, plays a vital role in protecting downstream cities and towns from floodwaters. All of the floodplains and wetlands of the Connecticut River watershed function as natural-valley flood-storage areas. The largest of these is the 20,000-acre region extending from Windsor Locks to Middletown, CT. During floods, the water spills over a wide area, dissipating the destructive force of the current and depositing nutrients in the soil. Some of the water soaks into the ground, and the rest is temporarily stored until the floodwaters recede. The effect of natural-valley flood storage is to reduce the flood peak (the highest water level) as it progresses downstream. Reducing the flood peak reduces the destructive force of the flood and helps keep water out of the downtown areas of cities like Springfield, MA, and Hartford, CT.

In addition to the natural-valley flood storage, the U.S. Army Corps of Engineers has constructed 16 flood-control reservoirs on various tributaries in the watershed. However, it is interesting to note that the flood-storage areas in Massachusetts and Connecticut are 50% greater than the combined capacity of the 16 reservoirs. The importance of these natural-valley storage areas in protecting downstream communities cannot be overstated.

Over the last 100 years, some of this storage capacity has been lost, and more is being lost today. The most dramatic loss is from the construction of dikes that keep the floodwaters out of the floodplains. In this case, the water that otherwise would have spread across the floodplain must either move to adjacent areas – causing higher water levels there – or move on with the peak, causing increased flooding downstream. Filling in of the floodplain to raise structures above the flood level has the same effect. Paving over floodplains for parking lots and roads reduces the capacity of these areas to hold the water by preventing it from soaking into the ground. The water runs off more quickly, increasing the destructiveness of the flood and raising the peak level. The preservation of the natural-valley flood-storage areas is of critical importance in reducing the flood hazards throughout the watershed. ✦

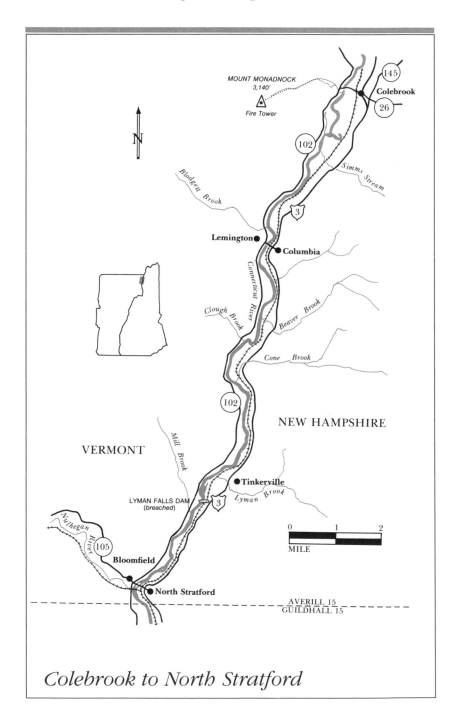

Colebrook to North Stratford

Colebrook to North Stratford

MILE FROM MOUTH:	363-349 (14 mile span).
NAVIGABLE BY:	Kayak, canoe.
DIFFICULTY:	Class I-II.
PORTAGES:	Lyman Falls Dam (breached), Vermont side,1/4 mile.
CAMPING:	No established sites.
USGS MAPS:	Averill 15.
EMERGENCY HELP:	Colebrook, NH (603) 237-5555, CB19. North Stratford, NH (603) 636-2353.

NOTE: there are no formal access sites between Columbia and North Stratford. The best bet for getting in and out is at the base of the Columbia and North Straford bridges.

Intermittent smooth water and Class II rapids characterize the River between Colebrook and North Stratford. Leaving Colebrook you'll find things much the same as they were upriver: a steady, peaceful current winding through pastures and fields with the wooded hills of Vermont and New Hampshire as a backdrop. A lone white farm house with a barn and silo stand in the distance and the sputterings of a tractor can be heard from somewhere just over the bank. During the spring and summer, a variety of bird life, including swallows, yellow warblers, crows, blackbirds, and robins, fly about the shore amid tangled driftwood and riverside trees. Not a bad way to spend an afternoon.

This type of scenery will continue until approximately 3 miles below the covered bridge connecting Columbia, NH and Lemington, VT. At this point the current begins to pick up and pastures give way to a thick wilderness scrub that lies close to the bank. Further on, you will begin to notice the River dropping in elevation and stretches of whitewater beginning to appear. A glance at your map will inform you that the Lyman Falls Dam is not far away.

The approach to the Lyman Falls area is misleading and dangerous since rapids extend all the way to the dam and there are no good warnings that a dam is ahead. Keep close track of your position, and look well downriver. When you see a number of log crib piers in the middle of the channel, head quickly for the Vermont shore and scout what lies ahead. The breached **Lyman Falls Dam** [352.5] can offer fun whitewater for the experienced paddler. The rapids at the dam are among the longest whitewater stretches remaining on the Connecticut River. However, numerous hazards must be watched for, including some steel rods sticking out of the dam. Proceed with caution and don't plan on running the dam unless you're prepared to swim. If you'd rather not go over the dam, get out on the Vermont side and portage around the whitewater.

Below the dam, watch out for boulders in the middle of the River. At mile 349.5 there is a "catch and release only" fly fishing area. From there, it's mostly swift water, with a few riffles to North Stratford, NH.

LOG DRIVES ON THE RIVER

Deforestation in the British Isles had long been a problem for the British Navy, which needed large trees for the masts and spars of its ships. The establishment of the American colonies provided a temporary answer to the problem, as the British Navy had exclusive right to the tall white pines. The Navy marked the trees with a symbol, and anyone found cutting a marked tree was severely punished.

However, the ousting of the British and the clearing of southern New England for farmland did not satisfy the demand for lumber. Trees from farther and farther north had to be cut and transported south. The easiest way to accomplish this was to float them down the Connecticut River. It was thought to be a rash idea to pass 60-foot-long logs through the Bellows Falls Gorge and other obstructions, but around 1879 the first major log drive brought down 3 million board feet of lumber to the mills in Massachusetts. Later drives would bring down 50 million board feet.

Log driving was a hazardous occupation. It began shortly after the ice went out while there was plenty of water in the River. Each year lives were lost on the drives, especially in dislodging the logjams. Some jams had to be picked apart by men balanced on floating logs. Other jams were so complete that they had to be blasted apart with dynamite. In later years, less tangle-prone 4-foot lengths were driven down the River. The drives arrived in Turner's Falls in August, having come perhaps 150 miles downstream over a

© *Connecticut River Foundation*

Loggers breaking up a log jam on the Connecticut River.

three-to-four-month period. The first major mill was at Riverside in Gill, MA. Other mills were established at Turner's Falls and Holyoke. At Holyoke a natural setback in the River made an ideal holding area for the logs and was the southernmost point of the log drives. By the 1880s the Holyoke area was one of the nation's leading producers of paper products.

The development of the railroads and highways spelled the end of the River log drives. Trucks and trains were able to transport the logs more quickly and less expensively. The last log drive on the Connecticut River was in 1915. ✦

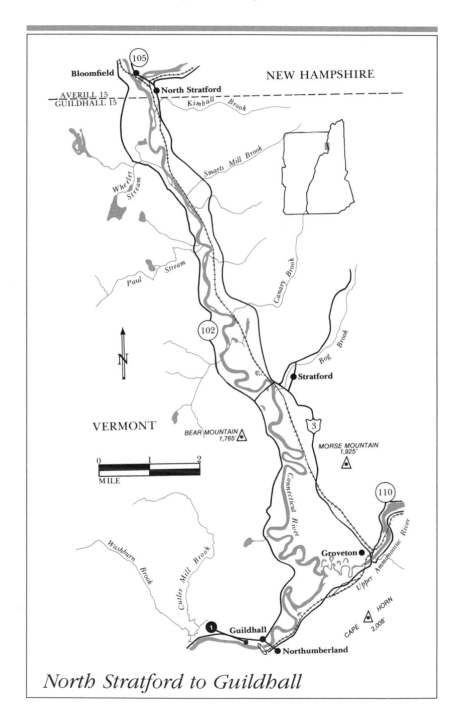

North Stratford to Guildhall

North Stratford to Guildhall

MILE FROM MOUTH:	349-326 (23 mile span).
NAVIGABLE BY:	Kayak, canoe.
DIFFICULTY:	Class I, quick water.
PORTAGES:	Mile 326, Northumberland Dam (breached), Vermont side, 1/4 mile.
CAMPING:	No established sites.
USGS MAPS:	Averill 15. Guildhall 15.
EMERGENCY HELP:	Stratford, NH (603) 236-2353.

The long stretch of River from North Stratford to the Guildhall Dam winds its way through farmland. Pastures run slowly up gracious hills in Vermont and abut sharply with hearty woodlands in New Hampshire, making this one of the more picturesque stretches of the River. Swallows and yellow warblers dance lightly on streams of air, catching bugs before landing in shore bushes or walking smartly along the muddy banks. The smells wafting from the fields constantly remind us that we are up-country. The River herself runs in lazy, wide turns, kept in check by high banks decorated with grass mantles that hang tenuously above the water, waiting for the eroding soil to fail.

Heading beneath the **North Stratford Rte. 105 bridge,** stay close to the Vermont shore to avoid rocks and shallow water. Just below the bridge, the **Nulhegan River** flows into the Connecticut from Vermont. The only access in this area is an informal landing about 1/2 mile below the bridge on the New Hampshire bank. Pull your boat onto the floodplain bank, and head into North Stratford for supplies. Until 1979, when ice floes destroyed them during the spring thaw, a number of houses stood on the floodplain below North Stratford.

Another mile below the bridge, the water passes over a steep pitch known as the "Horse Race." The water travels quickly here, but there are no real rapids, making the passage easy even for beginners. After the "Horse Race," the River widens and begins to meander, making for flat, slow water. Be sure to look for a glacial esker on the Vermont shore, its

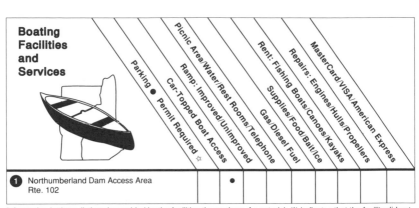

Boating Facilities and Services	Parking ●	Permit Required ☆	Car-Topped Boat Access	Ramp: Improved/Unimproved	Picnic Area/Water/Rest Rooms/Telephone	Gas/Diesel Fuel	Supplies/Food/Bait/Ice	Rent: Fishing Boats/Canoes/Kayaks	Repairs: Engines/Hulls/Propellers	MasterCard/VISA/American Express
1 Northumberland Dam Access Area Rte. 102				●						

Information in these listings is provided by the facilities themselves. An asterisk (*) indicates that the facility did not respond to our most recent requests for information.

James River Corporation paper mill at Groveton, NH.

bare sandy slope towering about 100 feet above the River. From here down to Guildhall, the River wanders in an aimless pattern of curves. You will see oxbows, sandy-point bars, and beaches. The high banks, eroding from the slow wash of River water, often conceal the lush, green pastures of neighboring farms. If you would like to take a brief side trip, **Paul Stream** enters on the Vermont side some six miles along. Canoes and kayaks can wander up this shallow stretch for a short way.

The bridge running between Stratford, NH and Maidstone, VT appears on the horizon after a turn in the River, and below that you may see where **Bog Brook** enters the River. The **Upper Ammonoosuc River** enters just

COOS COUNTRY

At Guildhall, Vermont, the Connecticut River enters into Coos Country, meaning "place of the curved river" in a local native American dialect. Coos Country extends some 100 miles south to White River Junction; this rich valley of fertile meadows and gently rolling hills edged by the White Mountains in the east and the Green Mountains in the west is often called the "Garden of New England."

The region is also known for the amount of lumber it has produced. The Kilkenny Railroad ran from the Kilkenny Mountains down through Lancaster, New Hampshire and carried 200 million board feet of lumber in the years 1887 to 1897.

On Labor Day weekend the tradition of an agricultural fair continues in Lancaster. The Coos and Essex County Fair features agricultural and livestock exhibits, horse and oxen pulling, a midway with rides, and all the other spectacles of a New England fair.

On the western slopes of the White Mountains, Littleton, New Hampshire is the commercial center of Coos Country. Still a prosperous little community today, Littleton peaked in the middle of the 19th century when it was a center for the raising of Merino sheep. In 1840, 617,390 sheep made their home in New Hampshire while 1,681,819 sheep slept in Vermont. This amounted to 2.25 sheep per native New Hampshirite and 5.75 sheep per native Vermonter. ✦

© *Embassy*

Local residents.

© Embassy

Northumberland Dam between Northumberland, NH and Guildhall, VT.

below Groveton, NH. Above its dam, which is quite an impressive sight, the Upper Ammonoosuc has many fine stretches of water for canoeists of varying skills: ranging from flat, slow water to fast rapids. From here, you can see the **Presidential Range** of the **White Mountains** to the east.

Before you reach Guildhall, there are some obscure back roads on the Vermont side which lead to spots close to the water. If need be, you could sneak in here and pull a canoe out of the water – just be sure to scout your locations beforehand and respect private property, even if it seems to be an abandoned cow pasture.

DANGER: *The Guildhall/Northumberland Dam is breached and quite dangerous. The waters here are not marked, and the current is often quite strong, so be especially careful to scout the approach from land. Do not attempt to run the dam, no matter what your skill.*

Take a good look at the James River Paper Mill in Groveton – this book is printed on paper made in that mill and then donated by the James River Corporation to the Connecticut River Watershed Council.

You can portage on the Vermont shore. Pull your boat up onto the rocky bank well above the dam and then carry it across the highway. Once on the other side of the highway, follow the edge of the woods until you are past the old cement power house and then head for the River. There is a clear spot with some sand that makes for a good put in, still on the Vermont side. 🏕️

CRWC Activities in Vermont

■ The Council has worked with other organizations to protect the Ottauquechee River from pollution resulting from intense development along its headwaters.

■ The Council has protected lands that are important for agriculture, forestry, wildlife, and fisheries.

■ The Council has developed a greenway management plan for the Ottauquechee River.

■ The Council has worked with state agencies and the legislature to establish strong protection for the state's upland streams.

■ The Council sponsors river-oriented special events and educational programs for the public.

■ The Council is conducting a River Watch program to monitor the water quality of the Connecticut River and its tributaries and to promote environmental education.

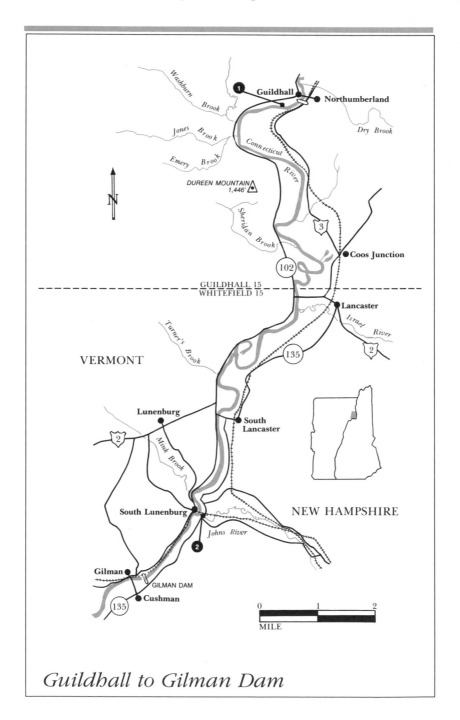

Guildhall to Gilman Dam

Guildhall to Gilman Dam

MILE FROM MOUTH:	326-302.5 (22.5 mile span).
NAVIGABLE BY:	Kayak, canoe (and small powerboats in stretches when the water is high).
DIFFICULTY:	Class I, quick water.
PORTAGES:	Mile 302.5, Gilman Dam, New Hampshire side, 1/4 mile.
CAMPING:	Mile 314.5, Prospect View Campground, Lancaster, NH (603) 788-4960, 788-2978.
USGS MAPS:	Guildhall 15. Whitefield 15.
EMERGENCY HELP:	Lancaster, NH (603) 788-4402. Gilman, VT (802) 892-7759.

The waters from Northumberland Dam to Gilman Dam are not so lonely as those covered in the previous chapter. The River still takes its time, wandering through long turns that fold into oxbows full of silent water and wildlife; but compared to the miles of farmland running from North Stratford to Guildhall, this section of River is diverse. At this point the boater will have premonitions of the population that will rear its head near Hanover, NH. In these miles, you will pass a dirt bank littered with old, abandoned cars. And if you continue south toward the Gilman Dam, the luxury of a small gravel ramp will greet you in South Lancaster, tucked between the railroad bridge and Johns River. Those who care for a short drive and a bite to eat should head to the Riverside Café in Gilman, where the food is hearty, the menu full, and the prices low.

The portage around the **Northumberland Dam** is quite a long walk. You can pull out at the rocky bank above the dam on the New Hampshire side and then cut around the cement power station until you reach the River, where there is an informal access area; or you can hunt along the road for any access to the River that isn't privately owned. A mile or so below the dam, just off the side of the road in Vermont, a sloping hill leads to a small stream, where you can put in a car-topped boat. Paddling from the stream to the River, you will pass beneath a high, stone arch of

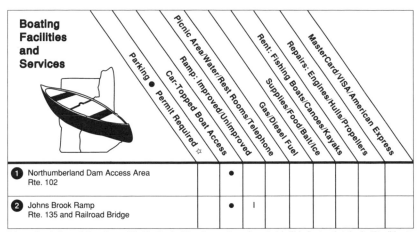

Boating Facilities and Services	Parking ● Permit Required ☆	Picnic Area/Water/Rest Rooms/Telephone	Car-Topped Boat Access	Ramp: Improved/Unimproved	Gas/Diesel Fuel	Supplies/Food/Bait/Ice	Rent: Fishing Boats/Canoes/Kayaks	Repairs: Engines/Hulls/Propellers	MasterCard/VISA/American Express
1 Northumberland Dam Access Area Rte. 102	●								
2 Johns Brook Ramp Rte. 135 and Railroad Bridge	●	I							

Information in these listings is provided by the facilities themselves. An asterisk (*) indicates that the facility did not respond to our most recent requests for information.

rusticated granite, long since abandoned. Trees are growing on top of the arch and your voice will echo loudly against the cut stone. From there back up to the dam, the River drifts through some wide, slow turns. From the arch south, you will find the River much the same – flat and slow, with little encouragement from the current.

Just below Northumberland Dam, you will pass high banks that show less erosion than those above. Birches, maples, and oaks lean over the water, holding the soil tightly against the River's clutch. These large trees keep the soil intact, and also drape the water with overhanging branches and leaves. Now and again, pasture appears, breaking the seamless embroidery of nature: the green fields linger wide against the uniform stretches of leaves and compliment the wilderness with a show of man's attempted order.

You will see many warblers, their small yellow breasts dancing against the uneven beat of the breeze, which itself normally runs north against the River's flow. Swallows also congregate periodically, swooping and gliding unharried over the tossing water, searching for bugs along the crests of wavelets. Both birds dart and slice into the wind with more control than seems possible, flying without heed to their own existence.

About six miles below Northumberland, you will pass a small oxbow on the west shore. If you have been running with a motor, pull it up before entering. The water at the mouth is shallow but deepens again once you're inside. The entire area is beautifully secluded. Wood duck nests, which are small wooden boxes nailed to the trees, range along the far shore and are maintained by NH Fish and Game. If you climb the banks you will find a large farm with many acres of pastureland.

Another 2 to 3 miles downriver brings you to the **Rte. 2 Bridge in Lancaster.** The current picks up as you pass the abutments but then slows back down. Below the bridge, the **Israel River** enters from the east bank. This water is too shallow for safe motoring, and the river mouth is tangled with large strainers, but a canoe could easily navigate through and continue up for a good stretch. The Israel River, in conjunction with **Johns River** below at South Lunenberg, was named for the Gline brothers – the first white men known to have wintered along these shores.

Continuing below the bridge, the banks begin to show increasing signs of erosion. Slabs of dirt fall into the River, making the water a muddy brown. Many farms along the River rely on natural and chemical fertilizers, and this sometimes makes the water too polluted for swimming. The run-off of fertilizers has been known to cause increased growth of water plants and algae, which can strangle a river. After an initial bloom, the plant life dies and falls to the bottom, depriving the river of oxygen as it decomposes. Though it has not occured near Lancaster, this state of hypoxia is sometimes the final step before a stretch of river dies.

From the **covered bridge in South Lancaster** downward, the River flows flat but with a stiff current. You will be facing an increasing headwind until you reach the dam. As you approach the railroad bridge running to South Lunenberg, begin to look for a small ramp on the New Hampshire side. The ramp is gravel and sits right between the bridge and Johns Brook. This is a good spot to put in a trailered boat, though there isn't much parking available.

Continuing south, you will approach the **Gilman Dam,** operated by the Simpson Paper Company Mill sitting on the Vermont shore. A log boom will prevent boats from approaching too close to the dam, but still exercise caution. Portage around the dam runs on the New Hampshire shore. You will have to hike to reach the next informal access, below the dam. When embarking, beware of the stiff current. You may want to head downstream a few hundred yards before putting in. 🏕

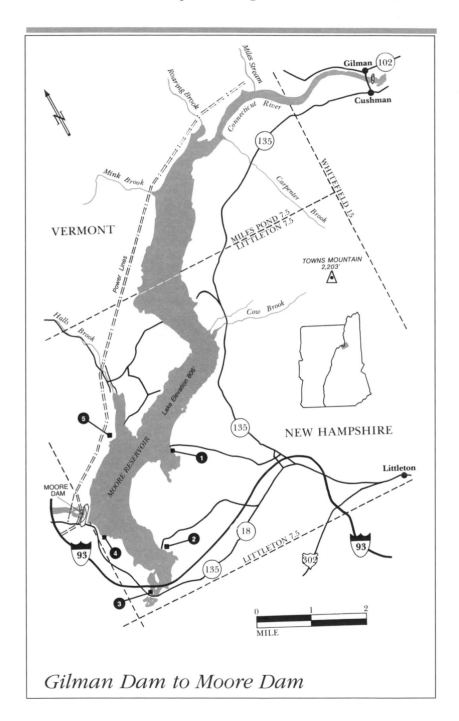

Gilman Dam to Moore Dam

Gilman Dam to Moore Dam

MILE FROM MOUTH:	302.5-291 (11.5 mile span).
NAVIGABLE BY:	Kayak, canoe; small powerboats and sailboat on reservoir.
DIFFICULTY:	Class I, flat water.
PORTAGES:	Mile 288, Moore Dam, Vermont side, 1/2 mile.
CAMPING:	Mile 290, Crazy Horse Campground, Littleton, NH (603) 444-2204.
USGS MAPS:	Whitefield 15. Miles Pond 7.5. Littleton 7.5.
EMERGENCY HELP:	Gilman, VT (802) 892-7759. Litttleton, NH (603) 787-6911.

Before it was flooded, the riverbed below Moore Reservoir was part of a stretch of rapids known as **Fifteen Mile Falls.** Extending to the present-day Comferford Reservoir, the Falls was a veritable whitewater paradise, dropping 350 feet over its length amid jagged ledges, boulders, and fallen trees. Aside the Falls stood the now submerged mill town of Pattonville. During the 1920's, the town was purchased and levelled by NEP, which recognized the region's potential for hydroelectric power. The Moore Reservoir area was flooded in 1956 and occasionally, during times of low water, artifacts of the town are still found along the shore.

The water below Gilman Dam is swift and rocky. Beautiful pine and spruce trees tower above as the River eventually widens into Moore Reservoir. The Reservoir is approximately 10 miles long and 1 mile wide. During the early morning when the air is still, the water resembles a sheet of silvery glass. When the air is not so still, however, the Reservoir's sizable waves may cause difficulty to any boater – take heed of the weather conditions before going out. Perch, salmon, trout, northern pike, pickerel, and bass all populate these waters.

New England Power Company has built a number of launch sites around the Reservoir available to the public. All of these access areas are well-maintained and equipped with picnic tables, barbecues, toilets, and

Boating Facilities and Services	Parking ● Permit Required ☆	Car-Topped Boat Access	Ramp: Improved/Unimproved	Picnic Area/Water/Rest Rooms/Telephone	Gas/Diesel Fuel	Supplies/Food/Bait/Ice	Rent: Fishing Boats/Canoes/Kayaks	Repairs: Engines/Hulls/Propellers	MasterCard/VISA/American Express
1 New England Power Co. Ramp Old Waterford Road		●	●	I	P R				
2 New England Power Co. Ramp Crazy Horse Road		●	●	I	P				
3 New England Power Co. Ramp Rte. 18		●	●	I					
4 New England Power Co. Ramp Moore Dam Visitors Center		●	●	I	PW R				
5 New England Power Co. Ramp Town Highway 43		●	●	I	P				

Information in these listings is provided by the facilities themselves. An asterisk (*) indicates that the facility did not respond to our most recent requests for information.

plenty of room to run around. New England Power also has a Visitors Center (603) 444-2997 at Moore Dam which is open from May to October. The 2,920-foot long dam is a massive landmark, capable of generating 190,000 kilowatts of electricity and worth a visit. The 1/4 mile portage around the dam begins on the Vermont side and is well-marked. 🔳

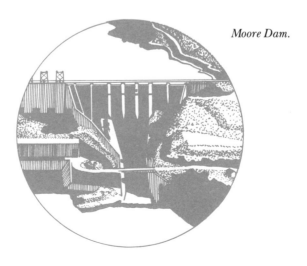

Moore Dam.

THE MOORE RESERVOIR

Prior to the construction of the Moore and Comerford hydroelectric power dams, the section of the Connecticut River from Gilman, VT, to the base of the Comerford Dam was known as "Fifteen Mile Falls." Cascading down among glacially deposited boulders, the River dropped almost 350 feet.

The 3,490-acre Moore Reservoir floods the falls. Behind the dam the water is 140 feet deep. The water intake valve for the power plant is 19 feet in diameter and causes water-level fluctuations of about 20 feet.

The reservoir is a popular area with boaters, and the scenery is beautiful. Yet beneath the surface, Moore Reservoir is in trouble. Plagued by water-quality problems since its construction, the reservoir is a virtual biological desert below a depth of 10 feet. The problem is a thick layer of organic sediment on the bottom of the lake discharged by the paper mill at Groveton, NH, and municipalities upstream prior to the installation of wastewater-treatment facilities. The decomposition of these organic sediments creates a biochemical oxygen demand (BOD) that uses all of the available oxygen in the water, leaving no oxygen for fish or plants. The problem is compounded during summer months by a layer of warm water on the surface of the reservoir that does not mix with the cooler, denser water down below. During the summer, oxygen from the surface never replenishes the oxygen used by the decomposing organic sediments on the bottom. The result is a total lack of oxygen below the surface layer and no place for the fish to go: the surface water is too warm, and there is nothing to breathe down below.

The problem is slowly being rectified by the construction of sewage-treatment plants and the installations of new wastewater-treatment equipment at the Groveton mill that will remove two-thirds of the BOD it generates. Though it may take some time for the accumulated sediments on the bottom to decompose, Moore Reservoir may one day be able to support year-round fish populations. ✦

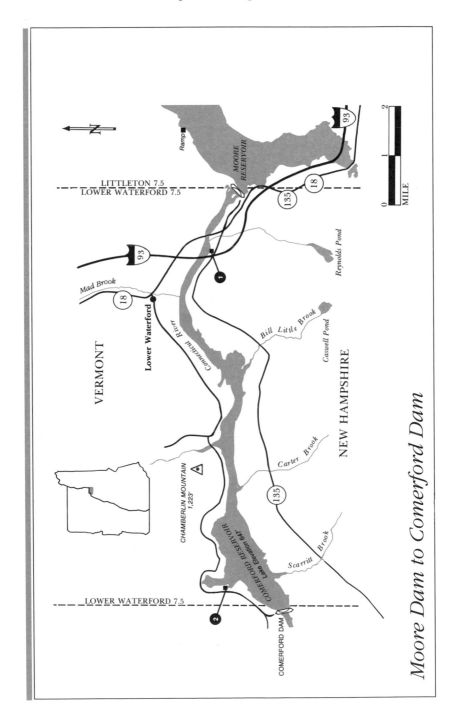

Moore Dam to Comerford Dam

Moore Dam to Comerford Dam

MILE FROM MOUTH:	291-284 (7.5 mile span).
NAVIGABLE BY:	Kayak, canoe, powerboats, and sailboats.
DIFFICULTY:	Class I, flat water.
PORTAGES:	Mile 284, Comerford Dam, New Hampshire side, 1/2 mile.
CAMPING:	No established sites.
USGS MAPS:	Lower Waterford 7.5.
EMERGENCY HELP:	Lower Waterford (802) 748-3111.

With Moore Dam to the east and **Comerford Dam** to the west, the Connecticut River resembles a quiet, narrow lake stretching beneath hills of spruce, birch, fir, and pine. Like Moore Reservoir, this area is peaceful during the calm of early morning when all you hear are the sounds of the surrounding forest. Loons, ducks, red-tailed hawks, bald eagles, herons, and a busy group of beavers all go about their affairs, generally unconcerned with passing vistors.

Beneath Moore Dam there is an access ramp between the Rte. 18 and Rte. 93 bridges. To get to it, simply exit Rte. 18 prior to crossing the River into Vermont. If you put in here, you may want to travel east to the base of the dam, just to get a sense of the immensity of this structure. Standing 178 feet high, Moore Dam is the largest on the River and when full, it holds back 3.3 million cubic yards of water within the Reservoir.

Moving west, **Mad Brook** trickles in from Vermont at mile 289.5. At this point, the River bends slightly south and at the base of the curve **Bill Little Brook** empties into the Connecticut from the New Hampshire shore. Many times, at the mouths of small brooks and streams such as these you will find rather elaborate beaver lodges and dams. The beaver lodge, home to a community of beavers, is usually an oven-shaped structure of sticks, grass, and moss, all woven together and plastered with mud. The lodge gradually increases in size each year with added repairs and elaboration. Dams, which consist of fallen trees, sticks, stones, and mud, deepen the water around the lodge, increasing manueverablity and making traveling easier. Most dams stand about 5 feet high and 3 feet wide

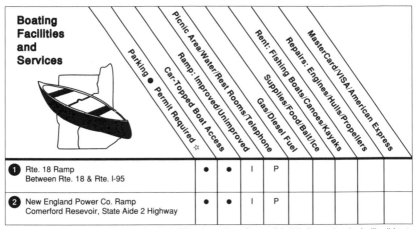

Boating Facilities and Services	Parking	Permit Required ☆	Car-Topped Boat Access	Ramp: Improved/Unimproved	Picnic Area/Water/Rest Rooms/Telephone	Gas/Diesel Fuel	Rent: Fishing Boats/Canoes/Kayaks	Supplies/Food/Bait/Ice	Repairs: Engines/Hulls/Propellers	MasterCard/VISA/American Express
1 Rte. 18 Ramp Between Rte. 18 & Rte. I-95	•		•	I	P					
2 New England Power Co. Ramp Comerford Resevoir, State Aide 2 Highway	•		•	I	P					

Information in these listings is provided by the facilities themselves. An asterisk (*) indicates that the facility did not respond to our most recent requests for information.

at the base, but some occasionally evolve into massive structures sprawling across a river or pond. In the Rocky Mountain National Park, CO, a dam more than 1000 feet in length was discovered.

Chamberlain Mountain stands on the Vermont shore just west of where **Chandler Brook** meets the River. Past Chandler Brook, you will be moving into the Comerford Reservoir and should be able to see Comerford Dam in the distance. Second in height only to Moore Dam, Comerford Dam towers 170 feet high and was built in 1930. There is a portage area on the New Hampshire side of the dam complete with a sandy beach and picnic areas. The trail leading below the dam is well-marked and approximately 1/2 mile in length. North of the dam, in a small, secluded cove on the Vermont bank, New England Power has provided a boat launch area which is well-equipped with shaded picnic tables, plenty of parking, and wide open spaces. 🌲

THE WHITE MOUNTAINS

Between Moore and Comerford dams one can see the Presidential Range of the White Mountains to the east. Mt. Washington, the highest peak in the Northeast, reaches 6,288 feet. The other peaks of the Presidential range are Mt. Jefferson, 5,725 feet; Mt. Adams, 5,805 feet; and Mt. Madison, 5,363 feet. The White Mountains are geologically different from the Green Mountains and the rest of the Appalachians. The White Mountains are the eroded roots of ancient volcanoes. Early explorers sailing along the New England coast could, on a clear day, make out the snow-covered summits, leading to their being called the White Hills, or White Mountains.

Providing little opportunity for farming and forming a barrier to travel, these mountains offered little incentive to settle in the area. In the 19th century the valleys and peaks of the White Mountains yielded a rich harvest of logs for the building and industrialization of America. However, the stripping of the forests exacted a heavy environmental price. Fierce fires and destructive floods followed the cutting of the forests.

In 1911 Congress passed the Weeks Act, sponsored by a native of Lancaster, NH, and authorizing the purchase of land to establish national forests, particularly in the eastern part of the country. One of the first national forests to be established was in the White Mountains. Today the land is managed under a multiple-use mandate. Timber products, water-resource protection, and recreation are the primary uses of the White Mountain National forests. ✦

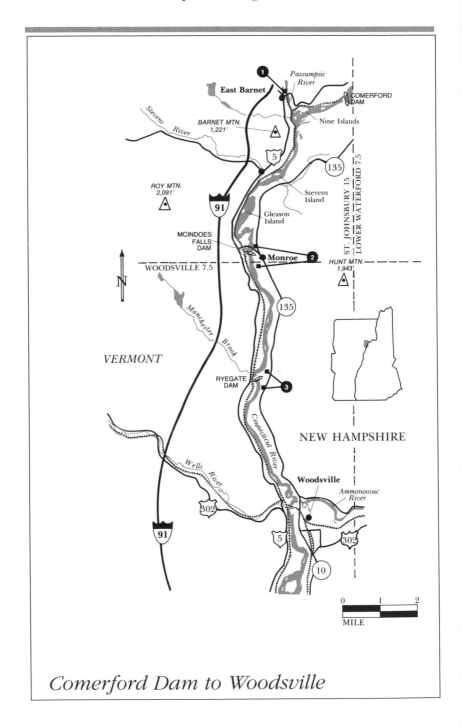

Comerford Dam to Woodsville

Comerford Dam to Woodsville

MILE FROM MOUTH:	284-268.5 (15.5 mile span).
NAVIGABLE BY:	Kayak, canoe.
DIFFICULTY:	Fast water, Class I-III, depending on the flow.
PORTAGES:	Mile 278, McIndoes Falls Dam, New Hampshire side, 200 yards. Mile 274, Ryegate Dam, New Hampshire side, 1/4 mile.
CAMPING:	Mile 269.5, Saddle Island, CRWC (603) 643-5672.
USGS MAPS:	Lower Waterford 7.5. St. Johnsbury 15. Woodsville 7.5 or 15.
EMERGENCY HELP:	Barnet, VT (802) 748-3111. Woodsville; NH (603) 747-3322. Monroe, NH (603) 638-2515.

The stretch of water from Comerford Dam to Woodsville is one of the most varied and attractive on the Connecticut. Traveling the entire distance, you will portage around two dams, maneuver through white-water rapids, and face the beauty of paddling the slow water below Ryegate. Old log cribs jut above the water's surface and wildlife, ranging from beaver and muskrat to moose, roams the shore. Great blue herons, swallows, hawks, and the ever-present warbler are also seen here, so keep your eyes peeled.

It is difficult to put in just below **Comerford Dam.** The waters are sometimes high and othertimes shallow, the current can be swift, and the bottom is always rocky. Talking to an expert who often canoes the River from here to South Newbury, we learned that the best place to put in is just below the dam on the **Passumpsic River.** Below Innwood Manor, there is a small turn-around on the Lower Waterford Road, which leads to the Comerford Dam. You may put in car-topped boats here, just be careful of the slope, which is rocky and sometimes slippery. At this point, the Passumpsic offers some of the finest canoeing around. Be sure to

Boating Facilities and Services	Parking • Permit Required ☆	Car-Topped Boat Access	Ramp: Improved/Unimproved	Picnic Area/Water/Rest Rooms/Telephone	Gas/Diesel Fuel	Rent: Fishing Boats/Canoes/Kayaks	Supplies/Food/Bait/Ice	Repairs: Engines/Hulls/Propellers	MasterCard/VISA/American Express
1 Passumpsic River Access Area Rte. 5			•						
2 McIndoes Falls Portage Area Rte. 135			•						
3 Ryegate Dam Portage Area Rte. 135			•						

Information in these listings is provided by the facilities themselves. An asterisk (*) indicates that the facility did not respond to our most recent requests for information.

watch out for a hairpin eddy, just below Innwood Manor, that can easily flip a canoe. The water travels fast through here, so you have to maneuver carefully and quickly to avoid the rocks and the heavy turbulence. The Passumpsic is generally narrower and swifter than the Connecticut, which carries more water; this means the banks are closer and easier to see, but it also means you have to be extra alert.

DANGER: *The water from Comerford Dam to McIndoes Falls is considered to be the most challenging along the Connecticut River; this also means that it is some of the most dangerous, especially when the Comerford Dam is letting out water. Depending on the dam's output, the water level can fluctuate as much as six feet. DO NOT CAMP on any of the islands in the River, or near the River banks. In the past, several campers have been swept away by the sudden rise in water level.*

After traveling the short stretch of the **Passumpsic,** there are several large islands in the middle of the Connecticut where the two rivers meet. These islands can be visited, but be on the lookout for rising water, and be sure to secure your boat tightly. If you are coming from below the Comerford Dam, keep a lookout for the entrance to the Passumpsic. The current seems to pick up only slightly, and if you're not paying attention you might pass the entrance without even a glance. It is rocky, however, along the west shore near the confluence of the two rivers. You will see log cribs along the Connecticut as you are traveling south, especially when the water is low. These square collections of logs were used to trap other logs traveling downstream, so that they could be counted and measured. Above **McIndoes Falls,** large steel loops were anchored deep in the granite boulders to secure the logs traveling downriver. Once you have passed **Stevens Island** and the entrance of **Stevens River** in Barnet, the Connecticut gets much wider and shallower. Watch out for rocks and be sure to stay on the outside of the curve.

Approaching **McIndoes Falls,** look for portage signs along the New Hampshire bank. You can approach close to the dam, all the while looking for the small walking trail that has been worn into the soil along the bank. Pull your boat out and carry it the few hundred feet over the dam. Then you will have to watch the rocky bank and search for an easy spot to put back in.

The section between **McIndoes Falls** and **Ryegate Dam** runs only about 3 miles and is much like that above. The water is fast and shallow, with a number of rocks. You may want to scout particular stretches from land before getting in the boat.

DANGER: *The approach to Ryegate Dam is not marked. Look for the sharp bend in the River, running from right to left, and listen for the roar of the falls as a warning that you are approaching the dam. You should also look for the smokestack of the mill, which is a good landmark at the dam. Stay close to the New Hampshire bank and take out right after the bend to avoid being swept over Ryegate.*

Portage around **Ryegate** on the New Hampshire shore, about 1/4 mile above the dam. The trail leads through a slightly wooded section and over some slippery rocks before terminating below the dam.

During the summer, especially on weekends, you may have trouble with low water below Ryegate. However, during the week water is released by the mill and the generating stations upstream, at which time you should be able to paddle steadily. In the spring, and when water is being released, there is a strong current below the dam, and the River is quite muddy for about a mile. From here south, the River is Class I paddling. The road frequently passes close along the Vermont shore, and the banks take turns between cornfields, mixed woods, and even some open pastures. For long stretches, however, the high banks keep you from viewing the landscape.

DANGER: *In spring, it is best to scout this entire stretch of River from the shore before attempting to boat it. The volume of water which passes through these narrow channels, especially once the Ammonoosuc River* *enters, often creates a dangerous current and treacherous standing waves. Your best course is to the outside curve.*

Approaching **Woodsville,** you may scrape the cobblestone-like bottom during the summer. The River bends sharply toward the New Hampshire shore about a mile above the town. In higher water, the stretch through Woodsville is Class II paddling. The current eddies around some large granite islands and takes severe swings that can easily turn the tail of a canoe and then flip it. Paddle hard through and keep the boat pointing forward. Because of the rocky shores and the tight passage, this stretch is known as **the Narrows** and is one of the more picturesque spots along the River. Fishermen will want to drop a line here, as a number of species are attracted to the deep, cold water and the heavy current.

After turning the sharp bend, you will see an island – two at high water – which is owned by the Connecticut River Watershed Council. This is a nice spot for camping, just be sure to pack out whatever you packed in. Beyond the island, the River bends toward Vermont. There can be standing waves here, where the large **Ammonoosuc River** enters from New Hampshire and the smaller **Wells River** enters from Vermont.

Approaching the dam on the Ammonoosuc from the Connecticut River, you will see a pretty covered bridge and a waterfall. This area looks like Maine, with the rocky shores and needle trees clinging to the banks for dear life. The water above the dam is good for canoeing.

McIndoes Falls during the spring log drive around 1907.

© Connecticut River Watershed Council

THE GREAT FLOODS

Over the years the Connecticut River watershed has been the site of a number of floods. High water rolls through after heavy rains, excessive snow melts, or a combination of the two. Floods have caused a great deal of damage throughout the valley, spurring individual communities to fund flood-control projects.

In November 1927, Vermont Governor John E. Weeks commented on one great flood by claiming that "it was the greatest disaster in the history of [that] beautiful state." It was estimated that a cubic mile of the Atlantic Ocean had been carried north and east by a stream of oceanic air and dumped in Vermont. All state rainfall records were shattered. Fifteen inches of rain was said to have fallen in the mountains. In the Connecticut River Valley, the White River watershed at White River Junction and the Passumpsic River Valley at St. Johnsbury were hit particularly hard.

In March 1936, a great flood hit New England. Resulting from heavy rainfall and an unusually quick spring thaw, the equivalent of 16 inches of rain flooded the northern watershed. Ice jams destroyed bridges throughout the valley and caused a diversion of waters across the low meadowlands of Holyoke, MA. At one point, ice floes and 10 foot watercrests threatened to destroy the dam at Vernon, VT. A small crew of utility workers and volunteers worked all night patching the dam until the floodwaters receded. The River rose 28.7 feet in Springfield and 37.6 feet in Hartford.

In September 1938, the great New England hurricane roared through the Connecticut River Valley causing more damage and loss of life than any other event in New England history. More than 600 people were killed, and property damaged totaled more than $385 million. Flooding was worst in the tributaries of Massachusetts, Vermont, and New Hampshire, but the greatest damage was done to the coast of Rhode Island, which bore the full brunt of the storm.

In August 1955, hurricanes Connie and Diane hit the New England coast. After Connie had passed, Diane let loose with 19.75 inches of rain in Westfield, MA, an all-time record in New England. ✦

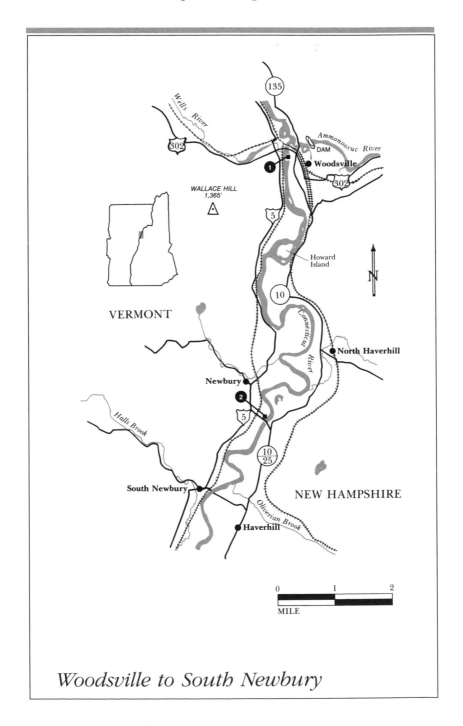

Woodsville to South Newbury

Woodsville to South Newbury

MILE FROM MOUTH:	268.5-255.5 (13 mile span).
NAVIGABLE BY:	Kayak, canoe.
DIFFICULTY:	Class I-II.
PORTAGES:	None.
CAMPING:	No established sites.
USGS MAPS:	Woodsville 15.
EMERGENCY HELP:	Woodsville, NH (603) 747-3322.
	Newbury, VT (802) 222-4680.

The Connecticut River around Woodsville looks as though it has been lifted from the pages of a naturalist's sketchbook. Heavy granite shores recede into the needles of softwood trees, looking like the country of the pointed firs. You will probably approach Woodsville by boat, leading directly from the stretch of River above, and the landscape will seem a welcome change from the constant view of muddy banks and cow pastures. Suddenly, you have a tough, eddying current created by the onslaught of a large tributary and the persistence of a rocky and gorged river bed. Be careful not to get sidewards to the current, as the powerful shifts in flow can easily tip a canoe. On the Vermont side, a tall steeple makes a good landmark just below the Wells River bridge.

The **Ammonoosuc River** merges with the Connecticut just above the town of Woodsville, NH. The dam at the mouth of the Ammonoosuc is large and picturesque, with a covered, wooden bridge just below it. The Ammonoosuc is fine for kayaking and canoeing, with long stretches of flat water punctuated by brief intervals of easy rapids.

Not far below the **bridge in Woodsville,** a side road parallels the River on the New Hampshire shore and leads to a sandy access point where cartopped boats may be put in. The waters rushing through this twisted stretch of granite are considered Class II, and you will face occasional ripples for quite some way. Once past Woodsville, the River widens and splits around a number of islands, the largest of which, Howard Island, would be nice for a picnic. The island may be passed to either side, though you should proceed slowly in the dry summer months.

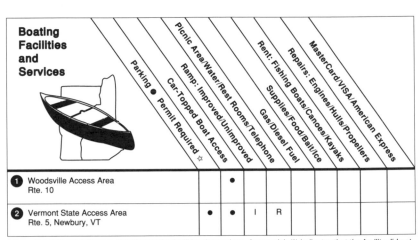

Boating Facilities and Services	Parking ●	Car-Topped Boat Access Permit Required ☆	Ramp: Improved/Unimproved	Picnic Area/Water/Rest Rooms/Telephone	Rent: Fishing Boats/Canoes/Kayaks Gas/Diesel Fuel	Repairs: Engines/Hulls/Propellers Supplies/Food/Bait/Ice	MasterCard/VISA/American Express		
1 Woodsville Access Area Rte. 10				●					
2 Vermont State Access Area Rte. 5, Newbury, VT	●	●	I	R					

Information in these listings is provided by the facilities themselves. An asterisk (*) indicates that the facility did not respond to our most recent requests for information.

Look for birds along both shores. In addition to the warblers, swallows, and red-winged blackbirds that have been present throughout the trip, we passed as many as six red-tail hawks at a time, soaring high above the line between the fields and the heavy stands of trees.

About 1-1/2 miles below Howard Island, the flat water begins to back up behind Wilder Dam. At an eastward sweep of the River stands **Placey Farm** on the Vermont shore. A large dairy farm with spectacular pastures and many cows, Placey Farm is one of the more photographed sites along the River. You may want to get out and take in the view from Rte. 5, which passes nearby. From here to the Newbury access ramp just above the bridge, maintained by Vermont State Fish & Game, the River yields a good number of fish, including some healthy largemouth and smallmouth bass. Head up one of the side streams if you'd prefer to land a good size trout.

At one time, there was a stream-bank stabilization project on the New Hampshire side below the bridge. Various materials were used to protect floodplain agricultural land from erosion, a constant problem that is aggravated by the cutting of small shoreline trees, such as alder. There appears to be less erosion here than at other spots along the River, but it is difficult to tell what experimental materials were used to keep the soil in place. It looks like a healthy river bank.

The bridge between Haverhill and South Newbury is no longer standing. The stone abutments are all that remained after a heavy windstorm swept downriver back in 1979. Ironically, the bridge had just been reconstructed two months earlier. Just above the abutments, **Oliverian Brook** enters from New Hampshire. This narrow, shallow brook is enclosed by heavy vegetation and offers a fine opportunity for birding and fishing. 🐾

MAJOR ROBERT ROGERS AND THE RANGERS

Major Robert Rogers and 200 Rangers were sent out by British General Jeffrey Amherst to revenge the capture of two officers, traveling under the flag of truce, by the St. Francis Indians. The flag had actually been a ruse to get past French patrols, but that didn't soothe Amherst's indignation.

Rogers set out by boat from Crown Point on the southern end of Lake Champlain in New York. Since the French controlled most of the lake, the Rangers had to travel at night. By the time they reached the northern end of the lake, 59 men had been sent back due to injury or illness. Rogers then hid his boats and supplies, left a small watch party, and headed on foot through the wilderness to the Saint Lawrence River.

The French soon discovered his trail and sent 200 men in pursuit. At this time Rogers sent word to Amherst that supplies should be sent up the Connecticut River from Fort No. 4 to the mouth of the Wells River, "that being the way I shall return, if at all...."

Rogers attacked the village of St. Francis in the wee hours of October 6, 1759, killing, he believed, 200 Indians. The actual count was closer to 30. Taking any supplies they could, the Rangers headed back south, with more French and Indians in pursuit.

After facing nearly two weeks of freezing temperatures with few supplies, Rogers reached the Wells River only to find the still warm embers of a fire set by the rescue party, who had fled thinking Rogers and his band were Indians. "Our distress on this occasion was truly inexpressible," Rogers later said.

Rogers then took three of his remaining Rangers and headed downstream on a timber raft, promising to return with provisions in 10 days. Rogers lost the raft, and nearly his life, in the Rapids at White River Falls. The men had no axes and so were forced to build another raft by burning trees to the right length. They almost lost their lives again at Sumner Falls, before finally reaching Fort No. 4 in six days. Within 1/2 hour of his arrival at the fort, Rogers sent supplies north, which arrived on the day promised.

Of the 141 Rangers taking part in the attack, 92 returned. What began as a daring raid had ended as a reckless mistake. ✦

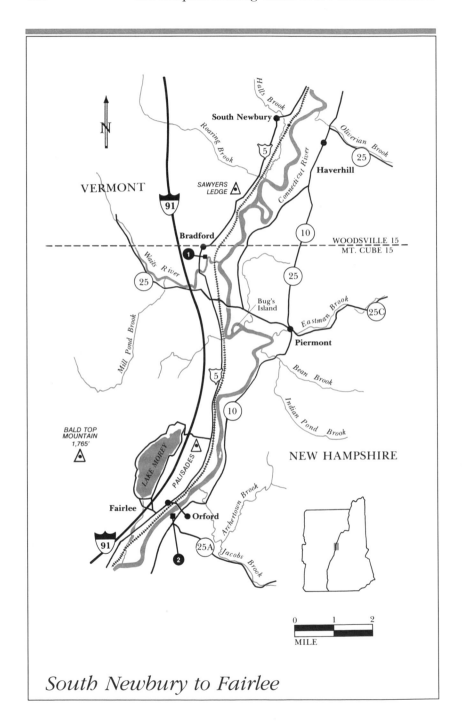

South Newbury to Fairlee

South Newbury to Fairlee

MILE FROM MOUTH:	255.5-239 (16.5 span).
NAVIGABLE BY:	Kayak, canoe; small powerboats (high water only).
DIFFICULTY:	Class I, flat water.
PORTAGES:	None.
CAMPING:	Mile 2385, The Pastures Campground, Orford, NH (603) 353-4579.
USGS MAPS:	Woodsville 15. Mt. Cube 15.
EMERGENCY HELP:	Bradford, VT (802) 222-4680. Piermont, NH (603) 335-4347.

M ountains, farms, and fish are order of the day between South Newbury and Fairlee. The River winds slowly southward, twisting occasionally to the east or west along steep banks where a herd of cows may stand lazily surveying the brown-colored waterway. Northern pike, bass, perch, and pickerel are all present here and a warm Saturday afternoon finds many folk out along the shore in hopes of a catch.

Heading downriver from South Newbury, past the abutments of the now defunct **Bedell Bridge,** the jagged peaks of **Sawyers Ledge** rise in Vermont just beyond Rte. 5 and the Boston & Maine Railroad. Directly across from the ledge is an oxbow cutoff with good fishing. In early spring, the surrounding green pastures, which rise and fall with the gentle slope of the valley, are speckled with bright yellow dandelions, making the whole countryside glow with contrasting color.

At mile 245.5 the **Waits River** empties into the Connecticut from the west just below the town of **Bradford.** The river derives its name from Captain Robert Wait who, along with his fellow Rogers Rangers (see page 111), took part in the famous 1759 attack on the St. Francis Indians. Just above the B&M railroad bridge on the Waits River is **Bugbee Landing,** maintained by the state of Vermont. Situated next to Bradford's Memorial Park and within walking distance of the town's store-lined streets, this is a useful place to stop and get supplies or simply browse around.

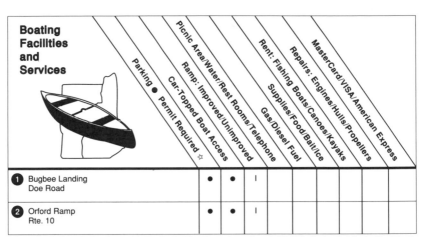

Boating Facilities and Services	Parking ● Permit Required	Car-Topped Boat Access ☆	Ramp: Improved/Unimproved	Picnic Area/Water/Rest Rooms/Telephone	Gas/Diesel Fuel	Rent: Fishing Boats/Canoes/Kayaks	Supplies/Food/Bait/Ice	Repairs: Engines/Hulls/Propellers	MasterCard/VISA/American Express
① Bugbee Landing Doe Road	●	●	I						
② Orford Ramp Rte. 10	●	●	I						

Information in these listings is provided by the facilities themselves. An asterisk (*) indicates that the facility did not respond to our most recent requests for information.

Below the Waits River confluence about 1/2 mile, you will pass under the Rte. 25 bridge. Gray in color, arching from bank to bank, and flanked by trees, the bridge is attractive and may inspire a picture or two.

Approximately a 1/2 mile below the bridge, the River bends sharply to the east where, on the Vermont side, a charming brook falls almost directly into the River. There is a good fishing spot on the opposite shore. If you continue to follow the bend eastward, **Bug's Island** will appear on your right, wooded, overgrown, and burgeoning with cattails. As you pass the island, the skyline of Piermont, NH, perched high above the riverbank, will gradually come into view. The **Eastman Brook,** which runs through the center of Piermont and makes its way down from the New Hampshire bluffs, trickles in at mile 242.5. As the River angles back toward Vermont, it gently glides between a number of looming masses of rock. **Sawyer Mountain, Echo Hill, Cottonstone Mountain,** and **The Palisades** all stand prominently along the River's perimeter.

The towns of **Fairlee** and **Orford** lie beneath the granite-faced Palisades. The bridge connecting the neighboring villages is much like the earlier Rte. 25 bridge, so if you regret not taking a picture then, chance has awarded you a second opportunity. Approximately 1/4 mile past the bridge on the New Hampshire side is a public access ramp. It is located immediately after The Pastures Campground which also has docking facilities – but you have to camp there to use them. On this stretch of river, in 1792, Samuel Morey (for whom the bridge and Vermont lake are named) successfully ran a steamboat between Orford and Fairlee 15 years before Robert Fulton launched his first steamboat.

If you have the time, both Orford and Fairlee are interesting small towns with a congenial air, pleasant surroundings, and plenty of restaurants – for those concerned about food. Orford has the added attraction of "The Ridge," which is a collection of seven stately, Federal-style mansions, built between 1773-1839, overlooking the River.

© Connecticut River Watershed Council

"Bulfinch Row" in Orford, NH.

ORFORD'S RIDGE HOUSES

In the 1830s Orford, NH was a prosperous community with a population of about 1,800 – roughly three times its present population. Washington Irving visited the town and wrote, "In all my travels in this country and Europe, I have never seen any village more beautiful than this. It is a charming place; nature has done her utmost here."

The seven Federal-style houses on the ridge above the Connecticut River are often called "Bulfinch Row" because they were thought to have been designed by the famous architect Charles Bulfinch. The Wheeler House, built in 1816, may have been designed by Asher Benjamin, an associate of Bulfinch, but the rest of the houses were designed by local craftsmen.

The first house on the ridge was built by Obadiah Noble in 1773 and was bought by Samuel Morey of steamboat fame in 1799. Morey made extensive renovations to the house, bringing it to its present appearance in 1804. It was here that Morey built and patented an internal combustion engine in 1826. In an attempt to prove that it could propel a carriage, Morey attached the engine to a wagon, which was propelled so quickly that it crashed into the walls of the workshop.

The other houses were built by local bankers, lawyers, and merchants. The last house on the ridge was built by Stedham Willard in 1839 and was apparently designed to rival the home of his father-in-law and next-door neighbor, Mr. Wheeler.   ✦

CRWC Activities in New Hampshire

■ The Council works in the State Legislature to establish protective programs for the watershed in New Hampshire. Land protection, recreation, and public access represent some of the issues which the CRWC has been actively involved with in New Hampshire.

■ The Council has provided funds to support research by graduate students and others on river ecology and related subjects.

■ The Council sponsors river oriented special events and education programs for the public.

■ The Council sponsors river-oriented special events and educational programs for the public.

■ The Council has worked to protect the last free-flowing reach of the Connecticut River at Sumner Falls from hydroelectric development.

■ Through its Conservancy Program the Council has protected lands that include forestland, important wildlife habitat, parks, and islands in the Connecticut River.

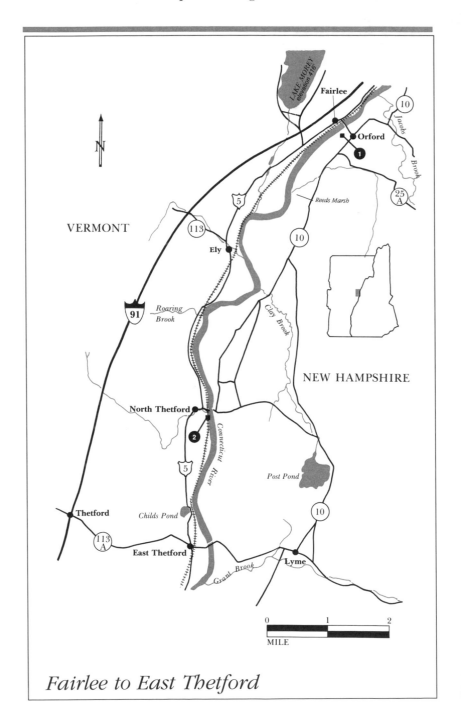

Fairlee to East Thetford

Fairlee to East Thetford

MILE FROM MOUTH:	239-230 (9 mile span).
NAVIGABLE BY:	Kayak, canoe, small power powerboat (high water only).
DIFFICULTY:	Quick water, flat water.
PORTAGES:	None.
CAMPING:	Mile 238.5, The Pastures Campground, Orford, NH (603) 353-4579.
USGS MAPS:	Mt. Cube 15.
EMERGENCY HELP:	East Thetford, VT (802) 353-4347. Hanover, NH 911.

Not surprisingly, the topography south of Fairlee is much like that to the north. The River roams slowly through fields and pastures, past cows, sheep, and barking dogs, twisting to east and west, and all the while surrounded by wooded hills and rocky crags. No doubt ducks, swallows, and the ever-popular crow will accompany you on your trek downriver, which, if in a canoe, may at times be difficult since the current here is slow and headwinds are sporadically channeled down from the mountains. Not to worry, though, this stretch of water is really quite enchanting and, at 9 miles, it is a less-than-strenuous paddle.

Leaving the Fairlee/Orford area the River is generally uneventful or peaceful – depending on your perspective. **Reeds Marsh** comes into view at mile 237.5 on the New Hampshire side. The River swings westward where it passes yet another marshy area – this one created by the runoff from **Lake Morey.** Continuing south, the town of **Ely** lies back from the shore on the Vermont side at mile 236. Below Ely about 1/2 mile, **Clay Brook** meets the Connecticut from the east after first flowing beneath a rustic covered bridge. If you paddle up Clay Brook, assuming water levels permit, you will come to a low marshy area slightly beyond the bridge which is good for birding.

There is a state ramp in North Thetford immediately following the abutments of a bridge which at one time connected the small Vermont town to the New Hampshire shore. The ramp offers ample parking and

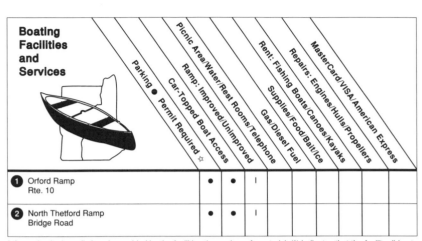

Boating Facilities and Services	Parking • Permit Required	Car-Topped Boat Access	Ramp: Improved/Unimproved ☆	Picnic Area/Water/Rest Rooms/Telephone	Gas/Diesel Fuel	Supplies/Food/Bait/Ice	Rent: Fishing Boats/Canoes/Kayaks	Repairs: Engines/Hulls/Propellers	MasterCard/VISA/American Express
1 Orford Ramp Rte. 10	•	•	I						
2 North Thetford Ramp Bridge Road	•	•	I						

Information in these listings is provided by the facilities themselves. An asterisk (*) indicates that the facility did not respond to our most recent requests for information.

is the only formal access site available between North and East Thetford. Further on, the B&M Railroad is visible along the Vermont shore all the way to **Childs Pond,** at which point the metal girders of the East Thetford bridge should come into view. 🎣

THE FIRST STEAMBOAT?

When travelers on the Connecticut River go under the bridge between Fairlee, VT and Orford, NH they pass the house of Samuel Morey, inventor of one of the first successful steamboats and of an internal combustion engine that predated Duryea's automobile engine. Yet, the encyclopedias all say that Robert Fulton invented the first successful American steamboat. The full story is somewhat more complicated.

One of the keys to success in steam navigation was the use of the side paddle wheel, which Morey used in a public demonstration in 1797. Through an oversight, Morey did not patent their use. However, Robert Fulton did in 1811, and from that time Morey could not legally use them.

Morey had turned his attention to improving the steam engine and applying it to the purpose of propelling boats as early as 1790. Morey described his steamboat as "about 19 feet long, 5-1/2 [feet] wide, and the engine occupies only about 18 inches of the stern, and sometimes goes between seven and eight miles per hour..."

In order to avoid an audience, Morey first tried out the dugout steamboat on a Sunday, when everyone was supposed to be in church. However, a few hookey players witnessed the launching from the New Hampshire shore. The boat ran with a paddle wheel at the bow and made about 4 miles an hour steaming upriver. The next time Morey ran his steamboat, the whole town came to watch.

Fulton probably knew of Morey's invention. During his summers in New York, Morey made contact with Chancellor Robert Livingston and interested him in his steamboat work. In 1797 he took Livingston on one of his boats, and Livingston promised Morey a "considerable sum" if he could make the boat go 8 miles per hour. Livingston also offered Morey $7,000 for the right to use his invention on the lower section of the Hudson River, but Morey turned him down. In June, Morey exhibited a side-wheel steamboat in Philadelphia. At some point the two men visited each other at their respective homes, but no agreement was ever reached.

In 1801 Livingston went to Paris, France and met Robert Fulton. Soon afterward the two men were granted a monopoly on steam navigation in New York State. They began work on a steamboat design, and in 1807 Fulton's steamboat made her historic voyage up the Hudson River, propelled by side paddle wheels.

Morey was a native of Hebron, CT who, in 1766, at the age of three years, came with his family to Orford by ox sled. The last 60 miles of the trip were made on the frozen Connecticut River because the Indian trail north of Charlestown, NH, was too narrow for the sled.

Morey's other engineering accomplishments included building the canal – locks, inclined planes, and dams – around the rapids in the Connecticut River at Bellows Falls, VT. In later years he moved to Fairlee, VT, where he died at the age of 80 in 1843. In 1890 he was recognized by the Vermont Legislature when the nearby Fairlee Pond was officially named Lake Morey. ✦

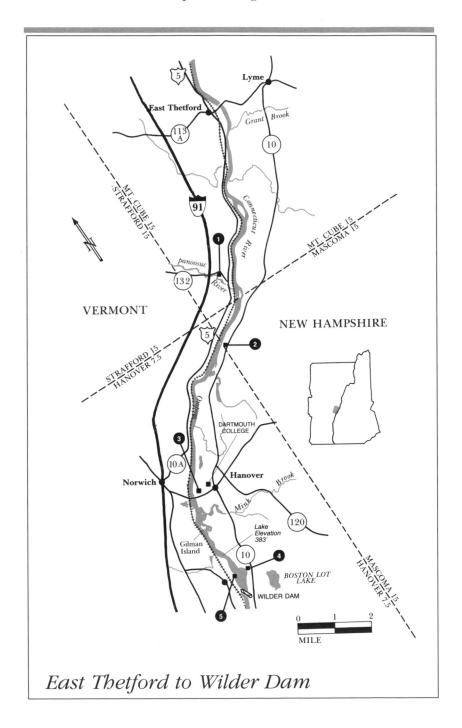

East Thetford to Wilder Dam

East Thetford to Wilder Dam

MILE FROM MOUTH:	230-215.5 (14.5 mile span).
NAVIGABLE BY:	Kayak, canoe, powerboats, and sailboats.
DIFFICULTY:	Flat water.
PORTAGES:	Mile 215.5, Wilder Dam, east side, 1/4 mile, (802) 295-3191.
CAMPING:	Mile 220, Chieftain Motel, Hanover, NH (603) 643-2550.
USGS MAPS:	Mt. Cube, 15. Mascoma, 15. Hanover, 7.5.
EMERGENCY HELP:	East Thetford, VT (802) 353-4347. Hanover, NH 911.

Between East Thetford and Wilder Dam, the barriers to suburban life finally give way. Woodland slips increasingly into the background as houses with manicured yards and planned accesses to the River begin to take over. The wilderness had disappeared several times before, only to return a short time later; however, Hanover marks a distinct change. From here on, the signs of people will subside from time to time, making room for nature, but not the other way around.

Still, this stretch of the Connecticut is beautiful, and the towns along the way are some of the most appealing in New England. Hanover itself is dominated by Dartmouth College, with huge greens and immaculate brick and whitewashed buildings sporting copper roofs. The woodlands around the college appear nearly pristine and are dominated by a mixture of hard and softwood trees.

Just below the bridge between East Thetford and Lyme, **Grant Brook** enters from New Hampshire. Below the Rte. 10 bridge, there is marshland and a state wildlife sanctuary with a number of birds.

Agricultural land, which has been asserting itself since well above North Stratford, gives way to a wooded shoreline. At mile 224, the **Ompompanoosuc River** enters from Vermont. Marshland follows as you head under the old railroad bridge at the mouth of the Ompom-

Boating Facilities and Services	Parking ● Permit Required ☆	Car-Topped Boat Access	Ramp: Improved/Unimproved	Picnic Area/Water/Rest Rooms/Telephone	Gas/Diesel Fuel	Rent: Fishing Boats/Canoes/Kayaks	Supplies/Food/Bait/Ice	Repairs: Engines/Hulls/Propellers	MasterCard/VISA/American Express
1 Vermont State Ramp, Old Rte. 132	●	●	U						
2 Wilson's Landing, Town of Hanover, Rte. 10	●	●	I	R					
3 Ledyard Canoe Club, West Wheelock Street (603) 646-2753	●	●		WR T		C K			
4 Lebanon Town Landing, Rte. 10 East Wilder Road	●	●	I						
5 New England Power Co. Ramp	●	●	I	R P					

Information in these listings is provided by the facilities themselves. An asterisk (*) indicates that the facility did not respond to our most recent requests for information.

panoosuc and continue beneath Rte. 5. A few hundred yards further, there is a set of old, stone bridge abutments and an unimproved ramp made of rocks and mud. The water leading to the ramp is particularly shallow. Maintained by the state of Vermont, the ramp is fine for putting in canoes and kayaks but not for trailered boats. You can reach the ramp by taking Rte. 5 to old Rte. 132, and there is plenty of parking.

About a mile below the Ompompanoosuc River, on the east shore, sits the Hanover town landing and dock. Called **Wilson's Landing,** the ramp is improved but covered with stones. There is a great deal of parking here, as well as public toilets. The ramp can be easily reached by way of Rte. 10. Continuing south be sure to notice the fine stone walls that run intermittently along the Vermont shore. Made of granite, some cut and some found, many of these walls have withstood nature's worst for a hundred or more years, all without the aid of mortar.

The steep and forested ridge along the New Hampshire bank 1 mile south of Wilson's Landing is the site of a glacial esker. An esker is a ridge of gravel deposited along a glacial ice sheet. Part of this area, kept by the Pine Park Association, has hiking trails, though camping is not allowed.

A dock and canoe rentals are available at **Dartmouth College's Ledyard Canoe Club** in Hanover. Both women's and men's crew teams race on this stretch of River during the spring and fall, so be extra cautious of your wake. If you're in a canoe, try to give the shells a run for their money. You will also see a few single-person shells, called sculls, and a number of racing canoes in the area. The small ramp just across from the Canoe Club is privately owned and should not be used.

The **Appalachian Trail** crosses the River at the **Ledyard Bridge** between Hanover and Norwich, running into the mountains on either side. Just below the bridge is a small cove tucked in behind a railroad trestle. The waters are often shallow, making it impossible for most boats to pass; at other times, however, you can sneak into the cove, where you will find the **Montshire** (Ver*mont* and New Hamp*shire*) **Museum of Natural History.** The museum is open to the public and can be reached by the water. The displays are superior and should be seen by all. You may also want to head back over to New Hampshire and view Dartmouth's fine collection of art. Hanover is also a good place to pick up supplies or get a meal.

A 1/2 mile south of the bridge, below the entrance to **Mink Brook,** you can explore **Gilman Island.** Another 1/2 mile along is a nature area called **Chambers Memorial Park,** owned by the Connecticut River Watershed Council, which has nature trails for those who would like to stroll.

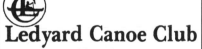

New England Power Co. has a picnic area at mile 214 on the Vermont shore and then a landing another mile further along, with a ramp made of concrete and protected by two stone walls. The water leading to the ramp is quite shallow, however; it is best to approach close to either wall. There are picnic tables, a large ballfield, and toilets available to the public. Across the River from this landing is the **Lebanon Town Landing,** with a paved ramp and garbage cans. This ramp can be reached via Rte. 10. From here, you will see **Wilder Dam** about 1/2 mile further downstream.

Wilder Dam was built on the site of **Olcott Falls,** where Robert Rogers and his famous Rangers watched their first raft shatter on the rocks in 1759, after having returned from attacking the St. Francis Indians. Today, New England Power Co. has a Visitors Center (802) 295-3191 at the dam, with a fish ladder and exhibits on energy and land conservation.

If you plan to continue your trip below the dam, take out on the New Hampshire side about 1/4 mile above the dam where there is a steep bank with wooden steps. You will see the trail near the picnic tables. The trail sits almost directly across the River from the power house and is separated from the picnic tables by Rte. 10. You will carry your boat along the Rte. 10 guardrail until you come to a grass and gravel road. The road will bring you past the old Visitors Center before winding along a fairly steep slope

to a set of stone steps to the River. The whole portage isn't much more than 1/4 mile long. Releases from the dam are made without warning, so be sure to secure your boat at the put-in, or it may be swept away by a sudden rise in water level.

You may also portage around the dam on the Vermont side. If you pull out above the dam at the NEP boat ramp, you can walk your boat to the Visitors Center parking lot and then head down to the "tail-race" behind the dam. Be extra cautious of the water flow on this side, however, as you are directly beneath the flood gates.

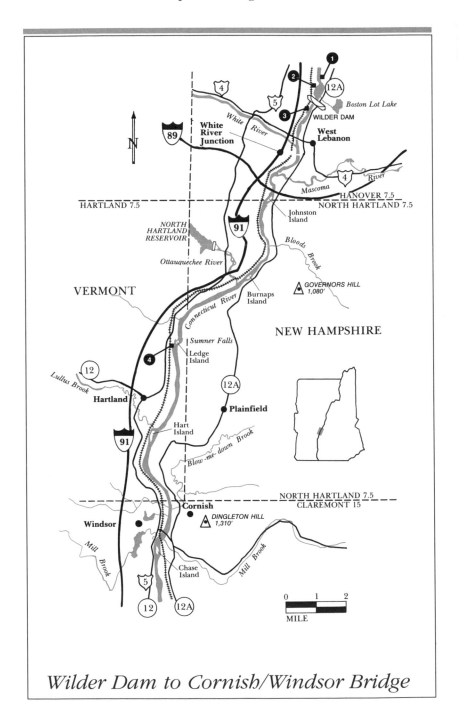

Wilder Dam to Cornish/Windsor Bridge

Wilder Dam to Cornish / Windsor Bridge

MILE FROM MOUTH:	215.5-199 (16.5 mile span).
NAVIGABLE BY:	Kayak, canoe.
DIFFICULTY:	Class I-IV.
PORTAGES:	Mile 206.5, Sumner Falls (Hartland Rapids), Vermont side, 1/4 mile.
CAMPING:	No established sites.
USGS MAPS:	Hanover 7.5. North Hartland 7.5. Hartland 7.5. Claremont 15.
EMERGENCY HELP:	Hanover, NH 911. Cornish, NH (603) 543-0535. Hartland, VT (802) 436-2600.

Beginning a trip at the Wilder Dam forces you to decide whether to brave the waters rushing over Sumner Falls. In the eight or so miles from the dam to the falls, you will face a variety of rapids and flat water. Depending on how much water is coming from the dam, experienced canoeists may want to try their hand at running the falls after some scouting from land. Putting in at the NEP access area below the falls and continuing downstream will bring you along a wide River bed with an influx of many other rivers and smaller tributaries. Other than the confluence of the White River, this stretch from Sumner Falls to Cornish should offer no problems to even the beginning paddler.

You will portage around **Wilder Dam** on the New Hampshire shore. Approaching the dam, you will see a large, stone-covered hill with a set of wooden steps almost directly across the River from the power house, which is on the Vermont side. Climbing the hill, you will see picnic tables just across Rte. 10 and then will walk along the Rte. 10 guardrail for a few hundred feet. A grass and gravel road will appear on the left and lead you past the old Visitors Center before a series of granite steps leads steeply to the water. Be sure not to approach the dam too closely while on the water, or you will face a chorus of reprimands from the people at the

Boating Facilities and Services	Parking ● Permit Required ☆	Car-Topped Boat Access	Ramp: Improved/Unimproved	Picnic Area/Water/Rest Rooms/Telephone	Gas/Diesel Fuel	Rent: Fishing Boats/Canoes/Kayaks	Supplies/Food/Bait/Ice	Repairs: Engines/Hulls/Propellers	MasterCard/VISA/American Express
1 Lebanon Town Landing East Wilder Road from Rte. 10	●	●	I						
2 New England Power Co. Ramp	●	●	I	P R					
3 New England Power Co. Access Area	●	●							
4 New England Power Co. Access Area	●	●		P					

Information in these listings is provided by the facilities themselves. An asterisk (*) indicates that the facility did not respond to our most recent requests for information.

power station, who are looking out for your safety. A boom will soon be placed above the dam to keep boaters from approaching too closely. Also be cautious of the current below the dam when you're putting in.

New England Power Company, which owns most of the dams along the Connecticut River – the others belonging to the beavers – has a new Visitors Center at Wilder Dam (802) 295-3191. The staff here will show you the new fish ladder, with its computerized gate system, and will give you information on hydroelectric power and its effect on the River.

Below Wilder Dam, the River is choppy for about 1/2 mile, especially when water is being released. Depending on the amount of water being released, you shouldn't have any trouble with a shallow bottom. The **White River** merges with the Connecticut about a 1-1/2 mile below the put-in spot, creating a swift current and heavy turbulence. The White River has extremely clean water and is therefore a prime spawning ground for Atlantic Salmon. Many fish stop here during their yearly migration while others continue upriver, aided by the fish ladder at Wilder.

White River Junction, VT is accessible by boat from Rochester, NY, depending on the water level after the spring freshet. You may want to head up the White River for a couple of miles to explore or to test your strength against the current. Below the abutments of the Rte. 91 bridge, there are two large boulders. There are picnic tables at **Riverpoint Park** near the confluence of the two rivers, where you can stop for a break.

Continuing down the Connecticut, you will have flat, quick water all the way to **Sumner Falls,** with a number of riffles here and there. There isn't much to see along the way, but this is a good stretch for paddling. You will cross a couple of small, Class II rapids that will excite the beginning paddler and liven the action for everyone else. Before you reach the **Mascoma River,** which enters from the east, there are two wastewater treatment facilities discharging into the River. Near the wastewater treatment plant in West Lebanon, along Rte. 12A, there is an informal access area for small boats. The Mascoma River is shallow but you may want to explore it for a short stretch, just for diversity.

From the Mascoma to the **Ottauquechee River,** the Connecticut River is quiet and isolated. You may see osprey, ducks, or even a beaver if you keep your eyes peeled. Pick your way carefully through the waters near **Johnston Island,** as the flow can be quite heavy when the water is high; on the other hand, when the water is low, you may have to get out and walk your boat. The land around **Bloods Brook,** which is owned by New Hampshire Fish and Game, is open to the public for fishing and hunting but not for camping. There is also a nice place to stop for lunch at the southern end of **Burnaps Island.**

If you head up the Ottauquechee River about 1/4 mile, you will see a covered bridge, a waterfall, and a small power plant owned and

operated by the White Current Corporation. Another mile up and the North Hartland Flood Control Reservoir (802) 295-2855 begins. The hydroelectric power plant at the 150-foot-high dam is operated by the Vermont Generation and Transmission Cooperative (802) 635-2331. There is a picnic area near the flood-control basin.

Below the Ottauquechee, there are two huge boulders known as **"Hen and Chicken Rocks."** These rocks mark the beginning of a stretch where the River is wider and much more shallow. Depending on the season, you will have to pick your way carefully to avoid scraping bottom.

DANGER: *Two signs reading "Danger – Falls Ahead" are located on the Vermont side about 1/2 mile above Sumner Falls, also known as Hartland Rapids. Listen for the roar of rushing water as you approach. At low water, you may not hear the sound until too late. More than one life has been lost here, so be cautious. If you choose to run them, scout the area from land first. Do not take a risk when the water is high.*

To portage around **Sumner Falls,** pull toward the Vermont bank as the River begins to swing to the east. From here, you can proceed cautiously to a rocky outcropping with a portage sign on the Vermont shore. You will have to walk along the rocks for about 50 to 75 yards and then climb a hill before reaching the short trail which leads through the woods to a dirt road and an NEP – maintained picnic area. From here, you will bear left on the road – which can be reached from Rte. 5, though it is easy to miss – and head downhill to a beach. Whirlpools

© *American Precision Museum*

The American Precision Museum in Windsor, VT.

THE AMERICAN PRECISION MUSEUM

Tools. There's hardly a basement, boat, or belfry that doesn't have some. And except for toolhardy people like machinists, mechanics, etc., almost everyone takes them for granted. In Windsor, VT, however, is a institution that takes tools very seriously, if not modestly, indeed. You'll find the American Precision Museum (802) 674-5781 at 196 Main Street.

Dedicated to hand and machine tools and their products, the museum is appropriately housed in an erstwhile armory and machine shop which dates back to 1846. At one time the building housed the most modern armory in the country, and produced army rifles with completely interchangeable parts – technology's cutting edge at the time.

By the mid-1960's the old brick armory was used only as a warehouse. Starting with a donated private collection of tools and an idea, the museum was incorporated in 1966. It operated part-time until 1977 when a professional director arrived and made it the best – and possibly only – museum in the country dedicated purely to the toolmaker's craft.

The collection on display has been privately donated, including everything from sewing machines to steam engines. There is even that most elusive and perplexing obsession of some inventors: a perpetual motion machine. Needless to say it doesn't work.

The museum is registered as a National Historic Landmark, and is open to the public from May 20 to November 1 for a modest admission fee, which you decide.   ✦

and fast current often gather in the little cove below the falls, so be cautious when putting in. Do not paddle back upriver from here.

Following the rapids, the channel is mostly straight with moderate flow between steep banks that limit your view. The River is isolated here with **Mt. Ascutney,** the highest peak in the Connecticut River Valley, dominating the view all the way to Hart Island. The channel running east around the island is wider but you will have to watch for rocks and some small pockets of rapids, depending on the water's height. The sandpits you see along the Vermont shore mark the site of an ancient glacial esker. The island is uninhabited and has no facilities but is a good place to stop for a rest. Young hardwoods and some scruffy brush line the banks.

Beyond **Hart Island,** the River gives up its privacy for a moment: the land opens, roads come into view, and even the trees look tamed. Between **Blow-me-down Brook** and the covered bridge at Windsor, the state of New Hampshire maintains an acess off Rte. 12A. You can walk from this area to the **Saint-Gaudens National Historic Site** in Cornish (603) 675-2175. While in town, you should also visit "The Oaks," home and studio of famous painter and illustrator Maxfield Parrish who lived from 1870 to 1966. Parrish was best known for his fairytale and romantic scenes which were inspired by the local countryside. Cornish was a popular summer resort in the early 1900s, and Woodrow Wilson kept his summer White House here in the years 1914 and 1915. Across the River, Windsor, VT was the site of the signing of the state constitution in 1777. The town is also a cradle of the machine-tool industry, whose history is captured at the American Precision Museum (802) 674-5781.

Running 460 feet, the **covered bridge between Cornish and Windsor** is the largest of its kind in the United States. As you approach the bridge, you will notice windows running all along its length; these, do not provide nearly enough light, however, so the bridge is also decorated with lamps inside.

© Connecticut River Foundation

The Cornish/Windsor Bridge over the Connecticut River. Built in 1866, the bridge is 460 feet long, making it the longest covered bridge in the country. The first bridge in this location was built in 1796 and was rebuilt three times until it was swept away in the flood of 1865.

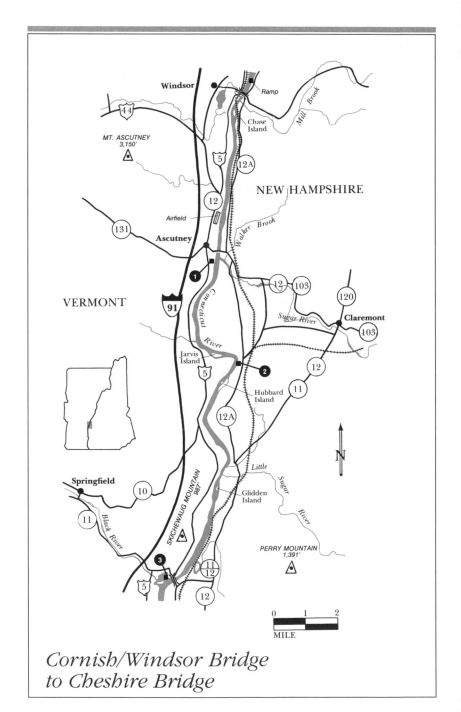

*Cornish/Windsor Bridge
to Cheshire Bridge*

Cornish / Windsor Bridge to Cheshire Bridge

MILE FROM MOUTH:	199-181 (18 mile span).
NAVIGABLE BY:	Kayak, canoe.
DIFFICULTY:	Class I, quick water.
PORTAGES:	None.
CAMPING:	Mile 194.5, North Star Canoe Rentals, Cornish, NH (603) 542-5802. Mile 192, Wilgus State Park, Ascutney, VT (802) 674-5422.
USGS MAPS:	Claremont 15.
EMERGENCY HELP:	Ascutney, VT (802) 674-2185. Cornish, NH (603) 543-0535.

From the Cornish-Windsor Bridge south to the Cheshire Bridge, the River is wide and flat, broken periodically by large islands and punctuated now and again by quick water with riffles. This is good water for paddling and as there are a few ramps along the way, fishermen may want to try a small outboard. Below Hubbard Island the sandy banks are teeming with cliff swallows and continuing past the confluence of the Little Sugar River, the air is full of blackbirds, swallows, and warblers.

Just below the covered bridge enter the two **Mill Brooks,** one from the east, the other from the west. Another 1/4 mile down, you will pass beneath the B&M Railroad bridge and see **Chase Island** ahead. At this point, the typical landscapes return, with pasture on the Vermont side and woodland in New Hampshire. South of Chase Island, which can be passed to either side, there is a private dirt ramp on the Vermont shore. A five mile straightaway, running almost due south, begins here. Watch out for a small, unnamed island that creeps up. Both banks begin to show spurts of erosion. Traveling along, you will have many fine views of the **Mt. Ascutney** foothills. You may camp in **Balloch's Crossing** at **North Star Canoe Rentals** (802) 542-5802, but please get permission first.

Routes 12 and 103 merge to cross the River toward the end of this long straightaway. Just below that bridge, on the Vermont side, you will see **Wilgus State Park.** This is a nice, little park located on a slope, with

Boating Facilities and Services	Parking ● Permit Required ☆	Car-Topped Boat Access	Ramp: Improved/Unimproved	Picnic Area/Water/Rest Rooms/Telephone	Gas/Diesel Fuel	Supplies/Food/Bait/Ice	Rent: Fishing Boats/Canoes/Kayaks	Repairs: Engines/Hulls/Propellers	MasterCard/VISA/American Express
1 Wilgus State Park Rte. 5 (603) 674-5422	●	●		PR W			C		
2 Ashley Ferry Ramp Rte. 12A	●	●	I	P					
3 Hoyt's Landing Rte. 11	●	●	I	R					

Information in these listings is provided by the facilities themselves. An asterisk (*) indicates that the facility did not respond to our most recent requests for information.

overnight camping, shelters, fireplaces, toilets, trails for hiking, and rental canoes. The unimproved ramp, which gets quite muddy after a rainfall, can be used to put in car-topped boats only.

The River winds along from here south, though there is only one dramatic turn in this whole stretch. Approaching this sharp bend, you will see **Jarvis Island,** covered with maples, oak, and other hardwood. Once past the bend, you will see the **Ashley Ferry Ramp** on the New Hampshire shore. Maintained by the Claremont Rotary Club in conjunction with NH Fish and Game, the ramp is good for putting in small boats and has a picnic area, all of which can be reached via Rte 12A.

Below the ramp at about mile 187.5, **Hubbard Island** sits splintered from New Hampshire. Covered with hardwood trees and lined with muddy banks, this island is big enough to attract all kinds of wildlife,

including birds and more elusive ground creatures such as raccoon. Below the island, the Vermont farmland reasserts itself. The River is flat and the going is easy from here to the Cheshire Bridge. Along the way, you will pass the entrance of **Little Sugar River,** with its fine collection of birds, and **Glidden Island,** which isn't much more than a blip on the screen of water. The **Cheshire Bridge** is one of the only toll bridges you'll see in these parts, but other than that, it doesn't stand out much. Just below it on the Vermont side, there is a small cove at the entrance of the **Black River.** In that cove is Hoyt's Landing, with a fine, small ramp and lots of parking. The area is kept very clean by the Vermont Fish and Game Department. The cove is rimmed with trees and makes for good exploring and fishing. Swallows abound in the cove; they seem to have cornered a large bug population and are busy harvesting them.

The final design of the Col. Robert Shaw Memorial, on Boston Common, commemorates Shaw and the Massachusetts 54th Regiment of black volunteer soldiers who served in the Civil War.

SAINT-GAUDENS NATIONAL HISTORIC SITE

River travelers interested in natural history and cultural diversion should visit the Saint-Gaudens National Historic Site (603) 675-2175 in Cornish, NH. The park is located on NH Rte. 12A about 9 miles north of Claremont, and is open from May through October.

The park is consists of the home, gardens, and studio of Augustus Saint-Gaudens (1848-1907), one of America's greatest sculptors. There are more than 2 miles of well-marked nature trails on the property, which was Saint-Gaudens' summer residence from 1885 to 1897 and his permanent home from 1900 until his death in 1907.

"Aspet," the sculptor's home, was once an inn along the stage road between Windsor, VT and Meriden, NH. During the summer of 1883, Saint-Gaudens began remodeling the house. Today, his furnishings are retained and demonstrate the character of the man and of his friends from the nearby colony of artists in Cornish.

Adjacent to the house stands the artist's studio. Near the studio are the gardens and the Gallery, which house many of Saint-Gaudens' works, including a replica of his famous sculpture, the *Puritan.* A short walk leads to the Ravine Studio and to the start of the Ravine Trail, a 1/4 mile walk along a cart path lined with wildflowers. ✦

Canoeing with the CRWC on the Connecticut River.

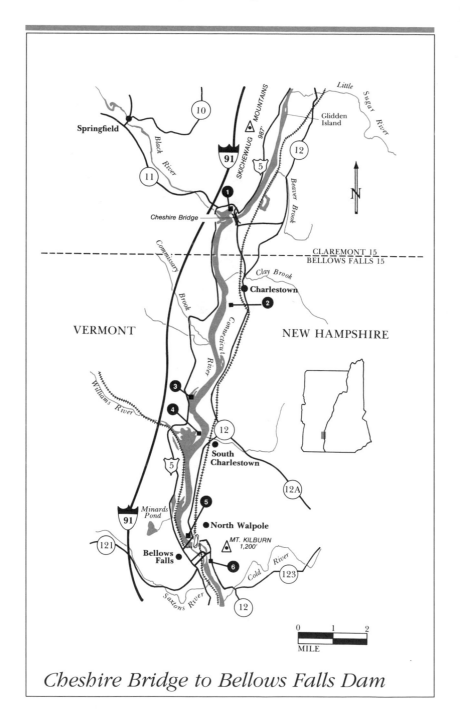

Cheshire Bridge to Bellows Falls Dam

Cheshire Bridge to Bellows Falls Dam

MILE FROM MOUTH:	181-170 (11 mile span).
NAVIGABLE BY:	Kayak, canoe, small powerboats.
DIFFICULTY:	Class I, quick water.
PORTAGES:	Mile 170, Bellows Falls Dam, NH side, 1-1/2 miles.
CAMPING:	No established sites.
USGS MAPS:	Bellows Falls 15. Claremont 15.
EMERGENCY HELP:	Bellows Falls, VT (802) 463-4528. Charlestown, NH (603) 826-5747.

The River runs wide and flat for most of the distance between the Cheshire Bridge and the Bellows Falls Dam. Shallow spots appear now and again, but for most of the way a good current pushes you quietly along. You may want to put in at the cement ramp off Rte. 5 below the Cheshire bridge. This is the first section of River where you will see a number of powerboats.

Just below the Cheshire Bridge stands a re-creation of the old **Fort at No. 4** (603) 826-5700. When constructed in 1745, the original fort was the northernmost English settlement in the Connecticut River Valley, and it played an important role in the French and Indian Wars. Camping is not allowed at the fort but facilities are available in the adjacent picnic area. Call the fort for more information and a schedule of events. You can tie your boat up at the bank below the fort and then walk up the hill to take a look – this is one site you don't want to miss.

Running along banks of green meadows, the River seems a graceful escort, carrying boaters where they wish to go. About two miles below the fort, on the New Hampshire side, New England Power Company maintains a landing known as the **Charlestown Recreation Area.** There is plenty of parking here, as well as toilets and a picnic site, but camping is not allowed. The landing may be reached via Rte. 12.

Another two miles along **Commissary Brook** meets the Connecticut from the west. The water near here gets shallow, especially during the

Boating Facilities and Services

Facility	Parking ● / Permit Required ☆	Car-Topped Boat Access	Ramp: Improved/Unimproved	Picnic Area/Water/Rest Rooms/Telephone	Boating Supplies/Food/Bait/Ice	Gas/Diesel Fuel	Rent: Fishing Boats/Canoes/Kayaks	Repairs: Engines/Hulls/Propellers	MasterCard/VISA/American Express
1 Hoyt's Landing, Rte. 11	●	●	I	R					
2 New England Power Co. Ramp, Charlestown Recreation Area, Rte. 12	●	●	I	P R					
3 Green Mountain Marine, Rte. 5 (802) 463-4973				PW RT	SF BI		FC K	EH P	
4 New England Power Co. Ramp, Herrick's Cove, Rte. 5	●	●	I	P R					
5 New England Power Co. Access Area, Pine Street		●	U						
6 Bellows Falls Dam Access Area, Rte. 12	●	●	U						

Information in these listings is provided by the facilities themselves. An asterisk (*) indicates that the facility did not respond to our most recent requests for information.

summer, so pass slowly and with your motor up. Two miles further and you'll see a large sign for **Green Mountain Marine** (802) 463-4973 perched on the Vermont bank. They should be able to make repairs and provide any marine supplies needed, and you can also rent canoes and small fishing boats. There is a steep, dirt ramp here, but it is open for use only to customers. Just below Green Mountain Marine, New England Power maintains a cement ramp at the **Rockingham Boat Landing** [173.5] (also known as Herricks Cove). There is plenty of parking and a number of facilities, including toilets, picnic tables, landing docks, and trash cans. The landing is accessible from Rte. 5. Continuing south, a large, shallow cove marks the entrance to the Williams River and is good for birding. The water is muddy here, and the bottom is too close for safe maneuvering with an outboard. A canoe can travel upstream for a distance, depending on the explorer's gumption.

Approaching **Bellows Falls,** the River narrows. Buildings are spread out on the west bank, looking like a magazine cover. The main street runs comfortably over the dam, merging North Walpole and Bellows Falls. Portage is on the New Hampshire side. Paddle along the east bank until you see a small inlet marked by an old red-brick building, where NEP operates a small picnic area. The steel I-beams you see are part of the flood-control system. From here, you will have to lug your boat around the dam to an access point 1-1/2 miles down Rte. 12. If you'd like a vehicle-assisted portage, call LHD Taxi (802) 463-9484 in advance.

Below the dam, a paved road runs off Rte. 12 to the water, where there's a sandy beach for putting in. You can wheel small trailers in by hand to put in a dinghy with an outboard motor. Be cautious of rocks in the waters just below the dam. The island has two bridges running to it and is the site of the **Bellows Falls Railroad Station,** which is an Amtrak stop but has no baggage pick-up and sells no tickets.

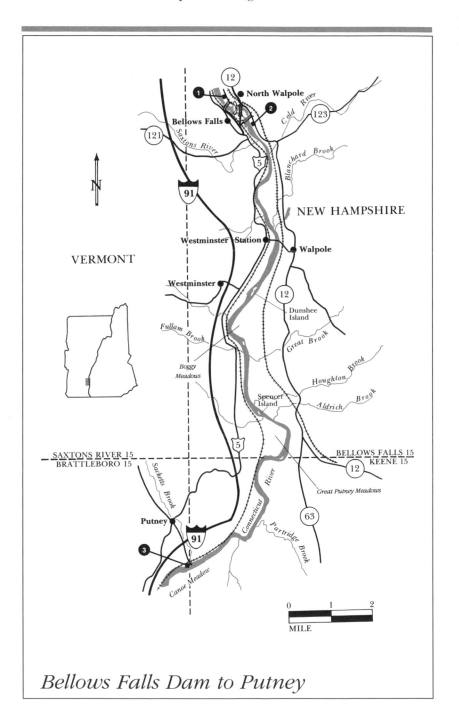

Bellows Falls Dam to Putney

Bellows Falls Dam to Putney

MILE FROM MOUTH:	170-153.5 (16.5 mile span).
NAVIGABLE BY:	Kayak, canoe, and small powerboat (high water only).
DIFFICULTY:	Quick water, flat water.
PORTAGES:	Mile 170, Bellows Falls Dam, NH side, 1-1/2 miles.
CAMPING:	No established sites.
USGS MAPS:	Bellows Falls 15. Keene 15. Brattleboro 15.
EMERGENCY HELP:	Walpole, NH (603) 352-1100. Putney, VT (802) 254-2950.

Though the River is now flowing through more populated regions, the landscape looks much as it did further north. Swallows dart along the banks with amazing dexterity, cows stand indifferently near the shore, patchy green and yellow pastures roll upward until they meet the timber of the surrounding mountains, and, of course, the distinctive scent of the barnyard colors the air. The towns of Bellows Falls and Putney may be a bit larger than their upriver counterparts, but the stretch between the two nevertheless exudes the same rural placidity.

From the New England Power Co. landing north of **Bellows Falls Dam,** the portage is about 1-1/2 miles on the New Hampshire side to the Rte.12 access area. You may also cross the bridge from North Walpole into Bellows Falls, turn left, go to the center of town, past Frank Adam's Grist Mill, and put in 1/4 mile below the mill. Bellows Falls has several sites of interest, including the Pennacook Indian carvings along the riverbank below the falls, the fish ladder and Visitors Center (802) 463-3226 at NEP's hydroelectric station, and the Bellow Falls Canal, now part of the power station. The first bridge across the Connecticut River was built at Bellows Falls in 1784 at the site of the present concrete **Vilas Bridge.**

Heading south on Rte. 12, the exit to the access area is easily identified by the hairpin right turn one has to make to get to it. If you're pulling a

Boating Facilities and Services	Parking •	Permit Required ☆	Car-Topped Boat Access	Ramp: Improved/Unimproved	Picnic Area/Water/Rest Rooms/Telephone	Rent: Fishing Boats/Canoes/Kayaks	Repairs: Engines/Hulls/Propellers	Supplies/Food/Bait/Ice	Gas/Diesel Fuel	MasterCard/VISA/American Express
1 New England Power Co. Access Area North Wapole, Pine Street				•	I					
2 Rte. 12 Access Ramp Rte. 12			•	•	U					
3 Putney State Ramp Old Ferry Road			•	•	I					

Information in these listings is provided by the facilities themselves. An asterisk (*) indicates that the facility did not respond to our most recent requests for information.

trailered boat, it may be wise to pass the exit, turn around, and come at the launch area from the south. After putting in, the **Saxtons River** empties into the Connecticut at mile 169 from Vermont. The mouth of the Saxton is unusually shallow so you might want to steer toward the far shore when passing. Two and a half miles downriver of the Saxton, the **Cold River** enters from the east. Legend has it that at one time the Cold River was so cold that the beavers built igloos instead of lodges. But that's only legend. If you're traveling this area during low water, keep to the Vermont shore to avoid scraping bottom.

At mile 165 the Rte. 123 bridge connecting **Westminister Station, VT** and **Walpole, NH** stretches across the River. Continuing southward another 1-1/2 miles, **Dunshee Island** comes into view and then New Hampshire's Boggy Meadows. On the Vermont side stands the town of **Westminister** whose Cumberland County Courthouse was the scene for a meeting of New York's British colonial administrators in 1775. American opposition to the meeting eventually led to the "Massacre of March 13, 1775" where two colonial protesters were killed. Westminister was also the place where "New Connecticut," later Vermont, was declared an independent state on January 16, 1777.

The riverbank along most of this area is steep and muddy. If you need to get ashore for any reason, try and find a sandy area or you will most assuredly sink to your ankles in mud. Passing by **Spencer Island** at mile 159.5 you will come to a large bend eastward known as **Great Putney Meadows.** This marshy lowland is a haven for birding generally and a particular favorite for great blue herons.

The remaining 6 miles to Putney are relatively smooth going. The steep, silty, muddy banks continue, as do the sprawling, tangly roots of riverside trees and the wire fences of neighboring farms. There is a public ramp at Putney which is accessible by Old Ferry Road next to the Putney Inn. The ramp is paved and there is parking, although manuevering may be tight for trailers. The town of Putney is 1/4 mile from the ramp and is well-fortified with grocery stores, shops, bed and breakfasts, and restaurants. Putney is also home to the annual Green Mountain Head Rowing Regatta for single and double sculling boats. The three mile race attracts rowers from around the nation.

HETTY GREEN

Vermont towns are replete with all sorts of unusual characters. A longtime resident of Bellows Falls, Hetty Green (1835-1916) inherited a large fortune from her father and managed it so shrewdly that she was considered the greatest woman financier of her time. Known as the Witch of Wall Street, her shrewdness was exceeded only by her stinginess. Her refusal to pay for medical care for her son, Ned, resulted in the subsequent amputation of his leg. She left an estate of $100 million (in 1916 dollars) and now rests in Immanuel Church cemetery. But she probably does not rest well, because Ned spent his fortune freely and was considered "as profligate as his mother was parsimonious." ✦

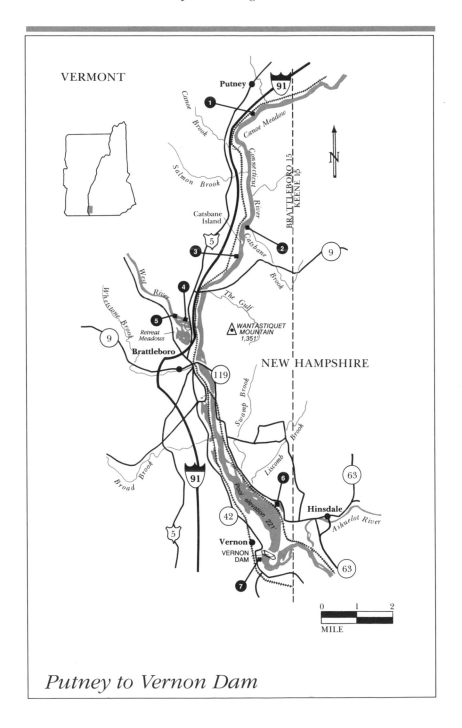

Putney to Vernon Dam

Putney to Vernon Dam

MILE FROM MOUTH:	153.5-138.5 (15 mile span).
NAVIGABLE BY:	Kayak, canoe, sailboats and powerboats.
DIFFICULTY:	Quick water, flat water.
PORTAGES:	Mile 138.5, Vernon Dam, Vermont side, 1/4 mile.
CAMPING:	No established sites.
USGS MAPS:	Brattleboro 15.
EMERGENCY HELP:	Brattleboro, VT (802) 254-2321. Hinsdale, NH (603) 336-7766.

Putney to Vernon Dam is the last stretch of River before leaving Vermont and New Hampshire behind. The banks continue to be steep and muddy, lined with pastures, fences, an occasional house, and are shaded by an increasing assortment of maple, ash, poplar, and oak. Departing from Putney, you will pass **Canoe Meadows** at mile 152.5 along the New Hampshire shore. Following the meadows there is a long straightaway ending at the confluence of **Catsbane Brook** [148.5]. **Catsbane Island** is downstream around the bend. The paved access ramp here has parking and is accessible by River Road in Chesterfield.

No less than a mile downriver, you will find another launch area, on the Vermont shore. With an asphalt ramp and plenty of room for maneuvering and parking, you should have little trouble getting to the River. The confluence of **The Gulf** is immediately south and then the River straightens out and heads directly toward Brattleboro.

At mile 146, the **West River** enters the Connecticut from Vermont. If you pass under the railroad and highway bridges and up the tributary, you will find numerous fishing and birding spots along **Retreat Meadows,** just north of Brattleboro. Connecticut River Safari (802) 257-5008, which rents and sells canoes, and the West River Marina & Restaurant (802) 257-7563 are across from Retreat Meadows and can fill both your eating and boating needs. The West River offers some of the best whitewater in New England and has been the site of the National Canoeing Championships. Spring and early summer are the best times to go.

Boating Facilities and Services	Parking ●	Permit Required ☆	Car-Topped Boat Access	Ramp: Improved/Unimproved	Picnic Area/Water/Rest Rooms/Telephone	Supplies/Food/Bait/Ice	Gas/Diesel Fuel	Rent: Fishing Boats/Canoes/Kayaks	Repairs: Engines/Hulls/Propellers	MasterCard/VISA/American Express
1 Putney State Ramp, Old Ferry Road	●		●	I						
2 Chesterfield Town Ramp, River Road	●		●	I						
3 State Ramp, Brattleboro, VT	●		●	I						
4 Connecticut River Safari, Rte. 5 (802) 257-5008	●		●		P T	S		C K		
5 West River Marina, Rte. 5 (802) 257-7563	●		●	I	R T			F		MV A
6 Hinsdale State Ramp, Prospect Street	●		●	I	P					
7 Northeast Utilities Hunt Recreation Center, Hunt Road	●		●	U	P					

Information in these listings is provided by the facilities themselves. An asterisk (*) indicates that the facility did not respond to our most recent requests for information.

The town of Brattleboro stands along the Vermont shore at mile 144. Named for town leader William Brattle, who moved to the area in the early 1720s, Brattleboro is a sizable municipality with many shops and restaurants, and is home to the Brattleboro Museum and Art Center (802) 257-0124. The **Rte. 119 bridge** between Brattleboro and the New Hampshire shore leapfrogs across the Connecticut River just upstream from the Georgia Pacific production facilities and the Boston & Maine railroad bridge.

From Brattleboro to the Vernon Dam, the riverbank becomes rural again with meadows and marshlands on both sides offering refuge to fish and fowl. The town of Vernon, noted for Fort Sartwell, built in 1739, and the Hunt House, home to Lt. Governor Jonathan Hunt, who served from 1794-96, is situated near the "great bow" in the River now occupied by **Vermont Yankee** and the Vernon Dam. Nearing the dam, Vermont Yankee's smokestack, reactor building, and cooling towers rise on the horizon. Groups wishing to visit Vermont Yankee should call the Energy Information Center (802) 257-1416 in advance.

Directly across the River from Vermont Yankee is a somewhat hidden state launch area in Hinsdale, NH. To reach this from the water you will travel beneath the railroad bridge and make an immediate right. The launch has a gravel ramp and plenty of parking. From land, the ramp is accessible from Prospect Street off Rte. 63.

Vernon Dam, owned by New England Power, began operations in 1909 with eight generators. Two more generators were added in 1921, thus bringing the station to its present 28,000-kilowatt capacity. Portage around the dam, which is neighbored by a beaver lodge, is on the Vermont shore next to the log boom. The trail, well-marked with portage signs, stretches about 1/4 mile around the dam to the **Governor Hunt Recreation Center** below. As you pass the dam, you will see the fish ladder which is open to the public during the shad and salmon runs from mid-May to mid-July. There are also two picnic areas along the trail with barbecue grills and tables. 🏕

THE MONTREAL EXPRESS

One of the worst train wrecks in New England history occurred just a few miles north of White River Junction. On the night of February 5, 1887, the last four cars of the Montreal Express derailed while crossing the bridge over the White River, sending 34 people to their deaths and injuring another 49.

The cars, made of wood, fell from the bridge to the frozen river and were set afire by the wood stoves used for heat. The wooden bridge also caught fire and was destroyed. The accident attracted nationwide attention and was one of the factors leading to the enactment of the Railway Appliance Act of 1893, the first national legislation setting safety standards for railroad equipment.   ✦

© *Connecticut River Watershed Council/Nacul Center*

The marsh lands along the Connecticut River provide an attractive environment for bird life. Here, two egrets prepare for flight.

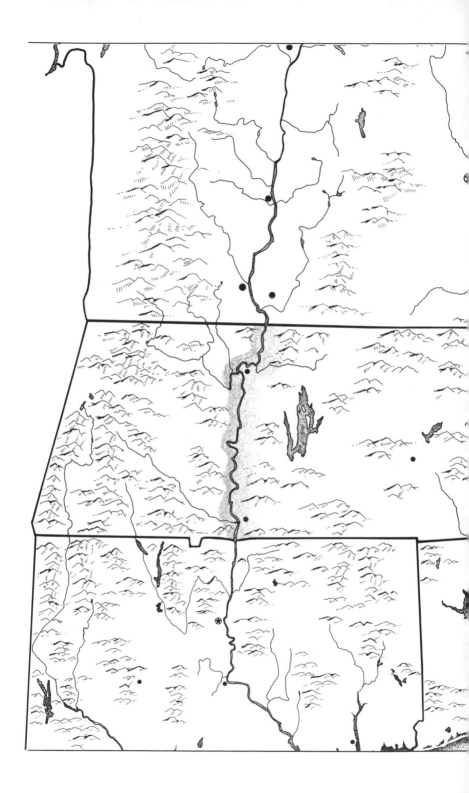

Massachusetts

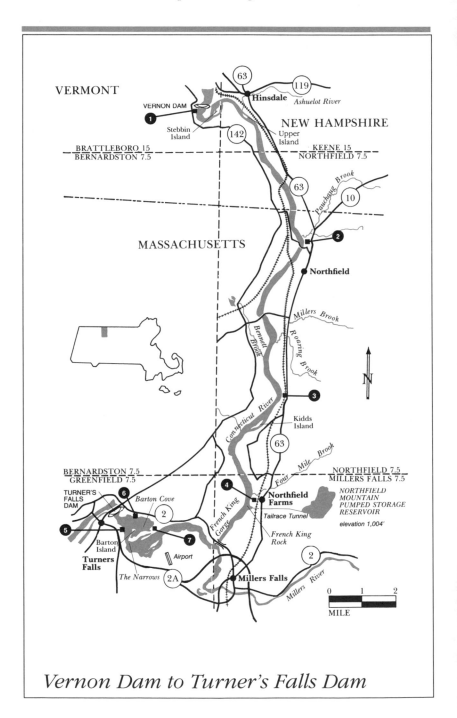

Vernon Dam to Turner's Falls Dam

Vernon Dam to Turner's Falls Dam

MILE FROM MOUTH:	138.5-117 (21.5 mile span).
NAVIGABLE BY:	Kayak, canoe, and small powerboats in pool above Turner's Falls Dam.
DIFFICULTY:	Quick water, flat water.
PORTAGES:	Mile 117, Turner's Falls Dam, Barton Cove Ramp, 4 miles.
CAMPING:	Mile 125.5, Munn's Ferry, Northfield, MA (413) 659-3714. Mile 119, Barton's Cove, Turner's Falls, MA (413) 659-3714.
USGS MAPS:	Brattleboro 15. Keene 15. Northfield 7.5. Millers Falls 7.5. Greenfield 7.5.
EMERGENCY HELP:	Northfield (413) 772-2133. Turner's Falls (413) 863-8911.

Chances are, you will find many a boater and camper along the River between Vernon Dam and Turner's Falls Dam. With wide and deep water, scenic vistas, camping facilities, nature preserves, picnic areas, and wooded trails, this leg of the River is a veritable wonderland for the outdoor enthusiast. The instigator of these alfresco pleasures is Northeast Utilities, who, having built a 300-acre reservoir and generating plant into Northfield Mountain, in turn, speckled the riverside with an extensive array of recreational centers that provide enjoyment all year around.

The **Governor Hunt Recreation Center,** right below Vernon Dam, is accessible via Governor Hunt Road off Rte. 142. A particularly good fishing area, the Center's launch area is sandy and maneuvering here may be tight since a number of trees stand near the shore. Once on the River, you'll notice the turbulence from the dam. Exercise caution. After making your way around the New Hampshire peninsula, **Stebbin Island** appears at mile 138. The island and surrounding area was popular with New

Boating Facilities and Services	Parking ● Permit Required	Car-Topped Boat Access	Ramp: Improved/Unimproved	Picnic Area/Water/Rest Rooms/Telephone	Gas/Diesel Fuel	Rent: Fishing Boats/Canoes/Kayaks	Supplies/Food/Bait/Ice	Repairs: Engines/Hulls/Propellers	MasterCard/VISA/American Express
❶ Hunt Recreation Center Governor Hunt Road	●	●	U	P					
❷ Pauchaug Brook State Ramp Rte. 63	●	●	I	P					
❸ Munn's Ferry Accessible from River only			U	P					
❹ Riverview Picnic Area Rte. 63	●	●		P R					
❺ Barton Island Ramp Rte. 2A	●	●	I						
❻ Barton Cove Ramp Rte. 2	●	●	I	PR T					
❼ Franklin County Boat Club Rte. 2 (413) 863-3006			PRIVATE CLUB						

Information in these listings is provided by the facilities themselves. An asterisk (*) indicates that the facility did not respond to our most recent requests for information.

England's Indians during much of the 17th century. They came to fish for shad and salmon, and plant the rich meadows. In 1676, the famous Waumponoag chieftain King Philip made the "great bow" his headquarters as he and other Indian leaders planned to attack the Connecticut Valley settlements downriver. There were few occasions in colonial history when so many native Americans were assembled in one place – approximately 2500. Below Stebbin Island is the confluence of the **Ashulot River** and **Upper Island.** There are several gravel bars between this area and the dismantled Boston & Maine Railroad bridge at mile 133, so be on the lookout.

The Massachusetts state line is at mile 132. The stretch of river immediately below the state line is flat, open, with slow water, and has five-to-six-foot banks that obscure views of the adjacent fields. You can take out at the state's **Pauchaug Brook Boat Ramp** in Northfield which is just north of the **Schell Bridge.** The town of Northfield is approximately 1-1/2 miles from the ramp and over the years has managed to retain much of its 19th century charm. Northfield's Main Street, known as "The Street," is even registered in the National Register of Historic Places.

Approximately 1/2 mile downriver from the Schell Bridge you will pass the Central Vermont Railroad bridge. The western bank, at this point, is green and lush, with high trees and swaying fields in the background. The low-lying **Great Meadow** bends out to meet the River from the east, and, as you continue southward, the **Bennett Meadow Bridge** appears at mile 128. Below the bridge on the west, lies the Bennett Meadow Wildlife Management Area which is part of the Northfield Mountain recreation system and a favorite of ducks, egrets, and great blue herons. Passing around a couple of gentle bends, you will find yourself at **Munn's Ferry** which provides picnicking and camping on a first-come, first-served basis. The Ferry can only be reached by boat and is equipped with an Adirondack shelter, five tent sites, water, and pit toilets.

Just downstream is **Kidds Island** at mile 125. **Pine Meadow** swells out from the eastern shore below the island and slightly beyond lies Northeast Utilities **Riverside Picnic Area** near Northfield Farms. Surrounded by tall, stately maples, oaks and pines, the picnic area is home to the *Quinnetukut II* riverboat. For a nominal fee, you may take a leisurely cruise exploring the history and geology of the region.

Directly behind the picnic area is **Northfield Mountain** with its 25 miles of scenic trails that double as cross-country-ski trails in the winter. Hidden deep within the mountain is a pumped-storage generating plant. During a period of high electrical demand, the water from the Northfield Mountain Reservoir is released to flow down through the pump turbines of the plant, thus producing electricity. The generating plant has the capability of producing one million kilowatts of electricity.

Immediately following the Northfield Farms area is **French King Rock** and the **French King Gorge** [121.5]. The Rock at the beginning of the gorge is enormous and can create heavy turbulence, even when the rest of the River is calm. Owing to the depth of the water, most of the Rock is submerged, so pass on either side close to the shore. As you enter the gorge, 250-foot walls stand to each side, and high overhead the **French King Bridge** stretches across the massive promontories. In late spring, the overhanging cliffs blossom with mountain laurel.

DANGER: *At the southern end of the gorge, the Millers River joins the Connecticut. In medium to high water, this confluence can be very rough due to both the volume and speed of the water.*

Where the **Millers River** joins in, the Connecticut makes a sharp turn to the west. The steep rock walls of the gorge gradually fall away as the

River widens near the Turner's Falls Dam. The landscape here in "the pool" is quite attractive. Tall pines, jagged inlets, and open water abound, as do ducks, gulls, osprey, herons, egrets, and sandpipers during the late spring. The reason this area is so attractive to birds is that the artificial tides created by the dam produce mud flats where the birds can easily find food. Be cautious, however, for these same artificial tides will displace your boat if it is not properly secured.

Proceeding through **The Narrows,** you enter **Barton Cove** [116]. On the south shore is a launch area with picnic tables and a cement ramp accessible by land via Rte. 2A. On the north shore of the Cove and along the peninsula is **Barton Cove Campground.** The Campground offers seasonal tent sites and rentals, as well as picnic areas, group canoeing, canoe and rowboat rentals, excellent nearby fishing, and a nature trail that includes an abandoned dinosaur track quarry. You may also want to look for one of the bald eagles that nest on the nearby islands.

The **Barton Cove Boat Ramp,** with parking, portable toilets, maps, and picnic tables, is located adjacent to the Franklin County Boat Club and is the pickup point for portaging around the dam – Northeast Utilities (413) 659-3761 provides free canoe portage service. To avoid delays, phone at least three days in advance of your planned arrival and request the shift supervisor. Call again when you reach the boat ramp. Canoeists and equipment are trucked to a put-in point below Northeast Utilities' Cabot Station hydroelectric plant.

If you wish to portage yourself, you should take out at the earlier mentioned town ramp on the south shore of Barton's Cove. Walk up First Street, turn left onto Main Street and pass the Farren Hospital. Turn left again onto Greenfield Road. Turn right onto Poplar Street just before the Montague City Bridge. You can put back in below the railroad bridge. The total length of the self-portage is about 3 miles.

Although it is not accessible from the River, you may want to make a special trip to see the fish ladder on the southern shore near the dam. The ladder enables migrating fish to circumnavigate the dam and reach their spawning grounds in the Upper Valley.

Any additional information regarding Bennett Meadow, Munn's Ferry, Riverside picnic area, Northfield Mountain, *Quinnetukut II* cruises, Barton Cove Campground, or Turner's Falls Dam can be obtained by calling Northeast Utilities at (413) 659-3714. 🔳

THE NORTHFIELD MOUNTAIN PROJECT

The Northfield Mountain Pumped Storage Hydroelectric Plant, owned by Northeast Utilities, is one of several electric generating stations using the resources of the River. The facility is unique, however, because it stores the potential to produce electrical energy in addition to generating it. Electricity itself cannot be stored. Water, however, and the potential to generate electricity with it, can be moved and stored relatively easily.

Water from the Connecticut River is pumped uphill to the top of Northfield Mountain. It is then allowed to run back down through turbines to generate electricity. Water is pumped up when electrical demand is low, usually at night or on the weekends, and the company has extra power from its other facilities. The water is stored in a reservoir near the summit of Northfield Mountain until the demand is high (perhaps in the late afternoon). Then water is released to supplement the company's generating capacity.

Northfield Mountain was selected for a pumped storage facility for several reasons. The metamorphic rock of the area is stable and provides the structural integrity needed for the tunnels and caverns. It is near the River and has a sufficient elevation to create an adequate hydrologic head to generate energy. The Turner's Falls Dam created a reservoir from which the water could be pumped and the terrain of the mountain's summit permitted the construction of an adequate storage reservoir near the top.

When the facility is operating, there are four pump/turbines that either pump water up to the storage reservoir or generate electricity from the water flowing down. When pumping, the water is drawn through the tailrace tunnel to the powerhouse. It is then pumped through the pressure shaft to the reservoir. Each pump can deliver 22,500 gallons per second. The reservoir has a capacity of about 5-1/2 billion gallons of water. When running in reverse, the pumps become generators and together have a 1-million-kilowatt generating capacity. ✦

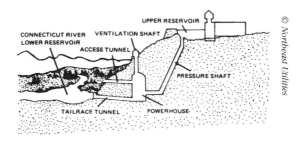

UPPER RESERVOIR
CONNECTICUT RIVER
LOWER RESERVOIR
VENTILATION SHAFT
ACCESS TUNNEL
PRESSURE SHAFT
TAILRACE TUNNEL
POWERHOUSE

© *Northeast Utilities*

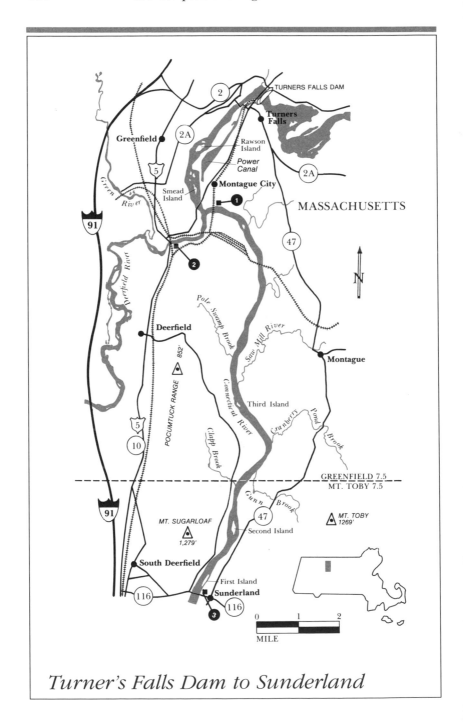

Turner's Falls Dam to Sunderland

Turner's Falls Dam to Sunderland

MILE FROM MOUTH:	117-106 (11 mile span).
NAVIGABLE BY:	Kayak, canoe.
DIFFICULTY:	Flat water.
PORTAGES:	None.
CAMPING:	No established sites.
USGS MAPS:	Greenfield 7.5. Mt. Toby 7.5.
EMERGENCY HELP:	Turner's Falls (413) 863-8911. Enviromental Police (413) 585-3247.

The shores are muddy between Turner's Falls and Sunderland. The River is slow, relatively straight, and lined with oaks, maples, ferns, cattails, and driftwood. Cormorants freqently perch themselves atop powerlines that cross the River and the whole region has a sort of lazy appeal. The access point at Poplar Street is strictly canoe or kayak. Underneath the Boston & Maine Railroad bridge there is a narrow, steep path leading down to the riverbank. Carrying anything other than a canoe or kayak to the water here is asking for trouble, not to mention a hernia. The River immediately below Turner's Falls is rough and and volatile due to releases from the dam. Do not camp or leave boats unsecured near the water's edge.

The **Deerfield River** [114.5] enters from the west directly across from the Poplar Street access area. A pleasant side trip is paddling up this tributary river to the historic town of Deerfield, site of the infamous Indian massacre of 1704. Deerfield has retained much of its colonial character and, under the auspices of Historic Deerfield Inc. (413) 774-5581, has refurbished twelve handsome 18th and 19th century houses which are open to the public. Adorned with distinguished grandfather clocks, ornately decorated chests, silver tankards, bright embroideries, and imported Chinese porcelain, these houses exude the look and feel of Deerfield's early history. There is an access area for canoes and kayaks only at the base of the Rte. 5 bridge.

South of the Deerfield River confluence, you will pass under the first of two railroad bridges that exist on this leg of the River. The banks are

Boating Facilities and Services	Parking ● Permit Required ☆	Car-Topped Boat Access	Ramp: Improved/Unimproved	Picnic Area/Water/Rest Rooms/Telephone	Gas/Diesel Fuel	Supplies/Food/Bait/Ice	Rent: Fishing Boats/Canoes/Kayaks	Repairs: Engines/Hulls/Propellers	MasterCard/VISA/American Express
1 Montague City Access Area Poplar Street	●	●	P						
2 Access Area Rte. 5		●							
3 Access Area Rte. I-91		●							
4 Sunderland Access Area Rte. 116 Bridge	●	●							

Information in these listings is provided by the facilities themselves. An asterisk (*) indicates that the facility did not respond to our most recent requests for information.

mostly wooded here, but occasionally the trees give way to a cultivated field. If you look to the west, you may catch a glimpse of the **Pocumtuck Range** which stands upwards of 800 feet above sea level.

Following the second railroad bridge [112] and a long straightaway, you will reach **Third Island,** which is owned by the Connecticut River Watershed Council and is available for camping. Further south is **Clapp Brook** [107.5] and on the west side of the River is **Whitmore's Ferry,** where in low water the Jurassic-age fish fossil beds can be seen. The Sugarloaf Mountains, so-named for their shape, stand off to the east. These pedestal-like peaks are remnants of a type of igneous rock known as Sugarloaf Arkose that covers most of the valley floor. If you are beginning or ending your trip on the Connecticut River at the Rte. 116 bridge, you may want to take a short detour up Mt. Sugarloaf for a terrific view of the Connecticut River Valley.

The Rte. 116 bridge appears after Mt. Sugarloaf, south of the **First Island.** From the boat launch on the east side of the River head 1/4 mile east on School Street into Sunderland Center for groceries.

The River between Sunderland and West Springfield is home to New England's only endangered species of fish, the shortnose sturgeon.

THE BLOODY BROOK, TURNER'S FALLS, AND DEERFIELD MASSACRES

In the fall of 1675 King Philip's War against the colonists reached the Connecticut River Valley when some of the local Indians allied themselves with King Philip, the sachem of the Wampanoags. The towns of Deerfield (Pocumtuck), Northfield (Squakeag), and Brookfield (Quaboag) were abandoned after Indian raids. The first attempt to evacuate Northfield met with disaster as Captain Beers and 36 men were ambushed and half of them were killed just 2 miles before they reached the town on September 4. On September 18, 80 men under Captain Lathrop were ambushed on the way back from harvesting the crops at Deerfield. The spot near the foot of Mt. Sugarloaf was afterward called "Bloody Brook."

After a winter of starving and on the run, many different groups of Indians gathered at Peskeommpscut (Turner's) Falls to fish, believing they were safe from attack. The commander of the garrison troops on the upper river towns, Captain Turner, heard of this and proceeded to the falls from Hatfield with 150 men on the night of May 18. He left his horse and crossed the river to one of the encampments, where his men shot into the wigwams of sleeping Indians, killing 100 to 300 Indians, mostly woman and children. Many fell or jumped to their deaths in the River or over the falls. Many Indians in nearby camps attacked the force in what became a panic-stricken rout back to Hatfield. One third of the men, including, Turner, were killed.

The Deerfield Massacre itself occurred 29 years later in 1704, when marauding Iroquois Indians attacked on New Year's Eve, destroying the town and killing or capturing all but a few of the 270 inhabitants. ✦

© *Connecticut River Watershed Council/Nacul Center*

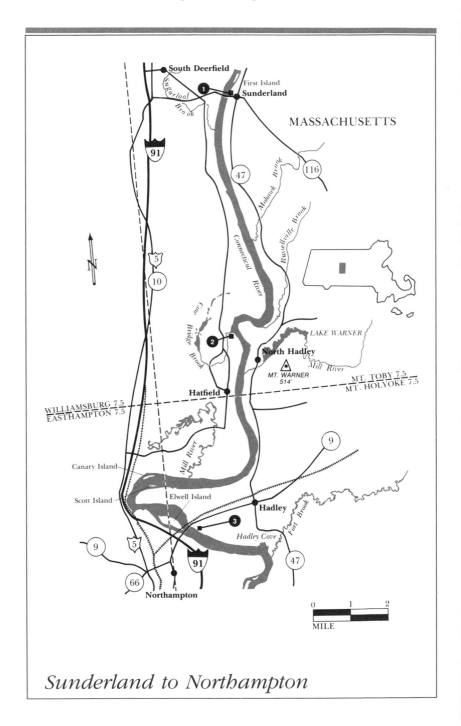

Sunderland to Northampton

Sunderland to Northampton

MILE FROM MOUTH:	106-92.5 (13.5 mile span).
NAVIGABLE BY:	Kayak, canoe, small powerboat.
DIFFICULTY:	Flat water.
PORTAGES:	None.
CAMPING:	No established sites.
USGS MAPS:	Mt. Toby 7.5. Mt. Holyoke 7.5. Easthampton 7.5.
EMERGENCY HELP:	Environmental Police (413) 586-3247.

The muddy banks continue as the Connecticut moves toward Northampton. Gliding slowly through the cultivated fields of the Pioneer Valley, the River here resembles a large expressway, stretching out for miles as it ambles through the countryside. Those in canoes or kayaks may want to stay close to the shore since large powerboats frequently zip down the center channel leaving behind a formidable wake.

From Sunderland, the River flows directly south. There are no rapids, no islands, no sudden turns, just straight, flat water for approximately 5 miles. **Mohawk Brook** enters from the east at mile 102.5, at which point, **Mt. Warner** will appear on the horizon in front of you. Further on, Russellville Brook trickles in where the River makes a 90-degree bend to the west. There is an access ramp at the mouth of **Cow Bridge Brook** just on the outskirts of Hatfield. To reach the ramp by car, drive 1-1/2 miles north on Main Street from the center of Hatfield. Look for a dirt road (Kellogg Hill) that veers toward the River as Main Street makes a sharp turn to the left. Cow Bridge Brook is a remnant of an earlier Connecticut River oxbow and is a nesting ground for ducks and heron.

Historically, the fertile meadows surrounding Hatfield and North Hadley have produced some of the finest shade tobacco grown in the United States. The broadleaf tobacco was grown under muslin tents to protect the delicate leaves from the sun, and was used exclusively to wrap cigars. However, due to the development of less costly means of production overseas, the tobacco fields have gradually disappeared.

Boating Facilities and Services	Parking ● Permit Required	Car-Topped Boat Access	Picnic Area/Water/Rest Rooms/Telephone	Ramp: Improved/Unimproved ☆	Gas/Diesel Fuel	Rent: Fishing Boats/Canoes/Kayaks	Supplies/Food/Bait/Ice	Repairs: Engines/Hulls/Propellers	MasterCard/VISA/American Express
1 Sunderland Access Area Rte. 116 Bridge	●	●							
2 Hatfield Ramp Main Street	●	●	I						
3 Sportsman's Marina Rte. 9 Bridge (413) 584-7141	☆	●	I	W R	G D	S I	C	EH P	M V

Information in these listings is provided by the facilities themselves. An asterisk (*) indicates that the facility did not respond to our most recent requests for information.

Today, strawberry, onion, and corn fields, as well as industrial parks and shopping malls have all but replaced the tobacco plantations.

Below the access ramp, the River remains straight for about 3 miles and then heads due west. The **Mill River** meets the Connecticut from the north at mile 94.5. **Canary** and **Scott Islands** lie just beyond the Mill River confluence and afterward the Connecticut makes a sharp U-turn cutting back east. Ducks, kildeers, and swallows continue to frequent the shoreline, and you may see a raccoon rustling in the underbrush. **Elwell Island** appears at mile 96 and is navigable on either side. Skipping across the tail end of the island is a railroad bridge and the **Calvin Coolidge Bridge,** Rte. 9, follows right on its heels at Northampton.

Sportsman's Marina (413) 584-7141 is to the immediate left after passing under the Rte. 9 bridge. The marina, which rents and sells canoes, in addition to being a full service boating facility, also allows canoeists access to the River with a permit. Permits can be purchased from the marina's front desk. A motel and restaurant are within walking distance behind the marina on Rte. 9.

A few miles to the east of this section of the River is the town of Amherst, MA, where Amherst College (founded 1821), the University of Massachusetts (founded 1863), Hampshire College (chartered 1965), and the Emily Dickinson House (413) 542-8161 are located. On the western bank of the River is the city of Northampton, home of Smith College (founded 1875) and President Calvin Coolidge.

THE NEW HAVEN
TO NORTHAMPTON CANAL

During the 1820s and 1830s, a fierce debate raged over how best to transport goods and people from the Connecticut coastline to central New England. Hartford and Middletown supported the improvement of the River with dredged channels, markers, and locks around the falls. New Haven businessmen, on the other hand, were jealous of all the trade traveling along the River.

Inspired by the success of the Erie Canal, they decided to build a canal from New Haven, CT to Northampton, MA. In 1822 a company was chartered to build the 75-mile-long, 60-foot-wide canal with some 60 locks to overcome the 520-foot change in elevation. The first boat, drawn by five horses, went the length of the canal in 1835. For a dozen years, the canal and the River steamboats were rivals and competitors. However, the canal suffered from inadequate capitalization as well as from droughts and poor construction, and was finally closed in 1847. ✦

© *Connecticut River Foundation*

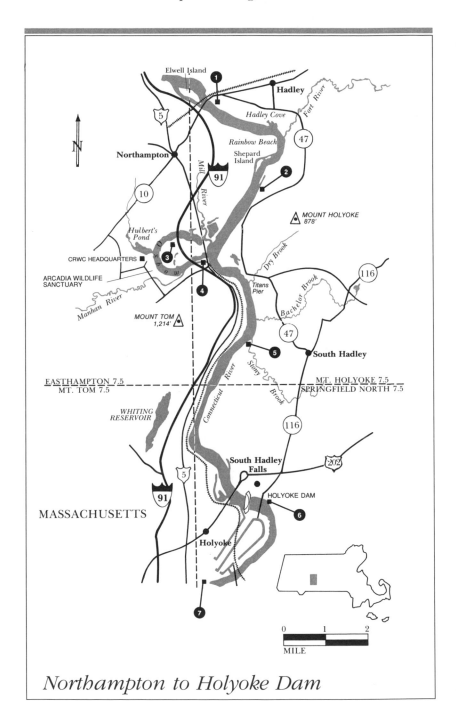

Northampton to Holyoke Dam

Northampton to Holyoke Dam

MILE FROM MOUTH:	92.5-81.5 (11 mile span).
NAVIGABLE BY:	Kayak, canoe, small powerboats, and sailboats.
DIFFICULTY:	Flat water.
PORTAGES:	Mile 81.5, Holyoke Dam, east side, 1 mile. Or vehicle assisted portage: Mile 85.5, Brunelle's Marina, east side, 4 miles, see text and call Holyoke Water Power Company during business hours (413) 536-9441, or (413) 536-9458/9449 at other times.
CAMPING:	Mile 90, Rainbow Beach, Northampton, MA.
USGS MAPS:	Easthampton 7.5. Mt. Holyoke 7.5. Mt. Tom 7.5. Springfield North 7.5.
EMERGENCY HELP:	Northampton, MA 911. Holyoke, MA (413) 536-0111. Environmental Police (413) 586-3247.

The 11 mile stretch from Northampton to the Holyoke Dam is one of the busiest sections of River north of Essex, CT. There are three good-size marinas here, and another below the dam. The Connecticut River Watershed Council Headquarters are in Northampton, behind the large oxbow and in the shadow of Mt. Tom; and only a short walk away is the Massachusetts Audubon Society's Arcadia Wildlife Sanctuary. Mt. Holyoke beckons from the distance, drawing hikers to its many trails for a spectacular view of the Pioneer Valley. You could keep yourself busy for a long time here, especially with the cultural activites at the area's five colleges – Amherst, Mt. Holyoke, Hampshire, U. Mass., and Smith. Even if you stay on the River, there are places to camp, watch birds, and relax in the sun. Not a bad place to visit, all in all.

Leaving the **Coolidge Bridge** between Hadley and Northampton, you will see **Sportsmans Marina** on the east shore. You can pick up gear for

Boating Facilities and Services

	Parking ● Permit Required	Car-Topped Boat Access	Ramp: Improved/Unimproved ☆	Picnic Area/Water/Rest Rooms/Telephone	Gas/Diesel Fuel	Supplies: Food/Bait/Ice	Rent: Fishing Boats/Canoes/Kayaks	Repairs: Engines/Hulls/Propellers	MasterCard/VISA/American Express
1 Sportsman's Marina, Coolidge Bridge (413) 584-7141	● ☆	●	I	W R	G	B I	C	E P	M V
2 Mitch's Marina (413) 584-9732	●	●	I	PW RT	G	I			
3 Oxbow Marina, Island Road (413) 584-2775	● ☆	●	I	PW RT	G D	FB I		EH P	M V
4 State Boat Ramp, Oxbow, Rte. 5	●	●	I						
5 Brunelles Marina, Alvord Street (413) 586-3132	● ☆	●	I	PW RT	G	SF BI		EH P	M V
6 Holyoke Dam Ramp, North Chicopee Street	●	●	U						
7 Jones Ferry Marina (413) 533-3996	●	●	I	PW RT	G	B I		EH P	M V

Information in these listings is provided by the facilities themselves. An asterisk (*) indicates that the facility did not respond to our most recent requests for information.

small boats here or use the ramp, though a permit is needed to launch and to park your car. Continuing south, you will come to **Hadley Cove,** a favorite feeding ground for heron, egrets, sandpipers, and ducks. Paddlers and small powerboats can explore the cove, though when the water is low, it would be best to keep an eye out for the propeller.

At the confluence of the **Fort River** – which enters from the east and can be explored by paddlers who don't mind climbing over, ducking under, and squeezing by strainers – the Connecticut takes a sharp turn south. On the west bank of the River is a fine camping spot called **Rainbow Beach,** named for the many colorful tents that blossom there each summer. Less than a mile from the beach, **Mitch's Marina** sits on the east bank. Mitch charges a small fee to use his launching facilities.

Below Mitch's, a 1-1/2 mile straightaway begins, along which the River is exceptionally wide and flat. At the end of this stretch, the **Mill River** would have entered just above the **Great Oxbow,** except that it has been diverted through **Hulbert's Pond** and into the Oxbow, to serve as the outflow from the Northampton Wastewater Treatment Plant.

Slightly further south, you will reach the **Manhan River,** which enters the Connecticut at the south end of the Oxbow. By passing under the railroad and highway bridges, you will enter the oxbow lake. There is a state boat ramp on the southern bank, just inside the railroad bridge. This ramp can be reached from Rte. 5. On the western side of the Oxbow, you can explore **Hulbert's Pond** – itself an ancient oxbow – and visit the headquarters of the **Connecticut River Watershed Council,** where you can grab a hot cup of java and listen to tales of life along the mighty Connecticut. You may also want to spend some time at the Audubon Society's **Arcadia Wildlife Sanctuary,** which has several nature trails and exhibits, as well as a library. **The Oxbow Marina,** a large and thorough affair, is located around the oxbow on the north shore. There is a launch here, accessible from Rte. 5 off Island Road.

The two most distinguished mountains in this area are **Mt. Tom** and **Mt. Holyoke,** both of which come by their characteristic shapes genetically – it is a natural form for mountains made of tough igneous rock. The asymetrical slope of the mountains comes from having been thrust violently upward along a deep fault line. The **Summit House** was built on Mt. Holyoke's summit in 1851. Guests rode up to the hotel on a horse-powered cog railway, in cars that were made from sleighs. Poets and artists have long ascended Mt. Holyoke to take in the fantastic, 360° view of the valley and the oxbow. Today, you can either drive up the mountain from Rte. 47, or hike the few miles on foot. You may want to land your boat at Mitch's Marina and walk from there.

A mile south of the Oxbow stands the coal-fired **Mt. Tom Power Plant,** operated by the Holyoke Water Power Company. Don't approach the plant from the water – the markers out front warning boats off should be heeded. The 200 foot cliffs of **Titian's Pier** stand opposite the power plant on the east shore, creating an impressive site from the water.

South of Titian's Pier is the entrance to **Bachelor Brook,** and 1/2 mile below that is the entrance to **Stony Brook** and **Brunelle's Marina,** which includes a year-round restaurant. This is the start of the vehicle-assisted, 4-mile portage around the Holyoke Dam, provided for free by the Holyoke Water Power Company (413) 536-9441. You should call the power company well in advance of your arrival to insure prompt and reliable service, and then call again once you reach the marina. Continue downstream if you would prefer a self-portage.

There are fossilized dinosaur tracks on the west side of the River at **Smith's Ferry,** less than one mile south of Stony Brook. Heading south, you will have to watch for ledges jutting into the River just below the spot where Rte. 5 reconnects with the water. Land at the access area at the foot of Old Ferry Road, and you will find the dinosaur prints in the shale outcropping between the highway and the railroad tracks.

Connecticut River Watershed Council

Water over the Holyoke Dam during a spring freshet in April 8, 1953.

DANGER: *At about mile 84, there is a beautiful stretch where the River narrows as it passes through a deep gorge. The water here is fast and rough. Stay well to the east, where there is more water and less turbulence.*

Nearly four miles below Brunelle's Marina, on the east bank, a small peninsula juts into the River; at the southern end of this point, the self-portage around Holyoke Dam begins. From here, you will ascend the tall bank to Canal Street in South Hadley and follow it until you are 1/4 mile below the **Rte. 116 bridge.** Under the bridge, there is a put-in beyond a small playground. The short ramp angles sharply off the road, and is not recommended for trailers.

Above the dam, the **Mueller Bridge** spans the River from South Hadley Falls to Holyoke. Above the bridge on the west bank, there is a natural holding area that was used by logging operations from the 1860s through the early 1900s. Logs cut in the north were floated downriver to supply the paper mills of Holyoke and were held in this basin known as **Log Pond Cove.** You can see murals of the cove at the Holyoke City Hall.

Holyoke Dam is not accessible by boat. A large boom with buoys warns boaters away from the dam well before actually reaching it. You may want to approach the dam (413) 536-5520 by foot, however, to see the fish lifts and other exhibits. The fish elevators have helped more than 4 million adult shad over the dam since 1955, so that they could continue their annual spawning migration north. The ladders and elevators are most active during May and June, and then again during the fall for the salmon run. You should call ahead to reserve a visitor's permit.

Finally reaching Holyoke, you may want to head into town for food or supplies. The city, which was the first planned industrial municipality in the nation, was designed to take advantage of the natural water power and to utilize the surrounding flatlands for factories and houses.

EMILY DICKINSON

Emily Dickinson (1830-1886) spent most of her life living as a recluse in Amherst, MA. During her lifetime, she published only seven poems. After her death, her sister found more than 1,000 other poems and arranged for their publication. A subsequent owner of the Dickinson house found even more poems in an old box in the attic in 1915. Today, Emily Dickinson is considered one of America's greatest poets. The Dickinson House (413) 542-2321 is open to the public.

Poem #49

I never lost as much but twice,
And that was in the sod.
Twice have I stood a beggar
Before the door of God!

Angels – twice descending
Reimbursed my store –
Burglar! Banker – Father!
I am poor once more! ✦

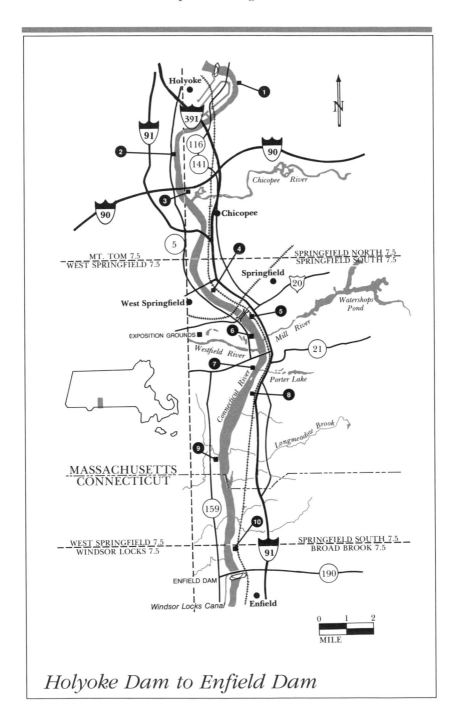

Holyoke Dam to Enfield Dam

Holyoke Dam to Enfield Dam

MILE FROM MOUTH:	81.5-63 (18.5 mile span).
NAVIGABLE BY:	Kayak, canoe, small powerboats; also small sailboats between Springfield and Rte. 190 bridge.
DIFFICULTY:	Flat water.
PORTAGES:	Mile 63, Enfield Dam, west side, 300 yards.
CAMPING:	No established sites.
USGS MAPS:	Springfield North 7.5. Mt. Tom 7.5. Springfield South 7.5. Broad Brook 7.5.
EMERGENCY HELP:	911.

The stretch from Holyoke Dam to Enfield Dam is perhaps the most industrialized section of the River. Lined with storm sewers, smoke stacks, powerlines, warehouses, and sewage treatment plants, the Connecticut here is a far cry from the pristine waterway of northern New Hampshire. Fear not, however, fellow admirer of the riverbank, for even here amid concrete, asphalt, and car exhaust there exist a few spots still blossoming with the splendor and beauty of nature. One particularly attractive characteristic of this area is the excellent fishing. During the shad run from mid-May to mid-June, as the fish are trying to make their way around Holyoke and Enfield dams, the River's shores are crammed with fishing enthusiasts – usually doing quite well.

About 1/4 mile below Holyoke Dam there is an unimproved access area on the eastern shore. Accessible via North Chicopee Street, this is a favorite fishing area during shad season. On any spring afternoon you'll find people of all ages and all walks of life cluttered together; some in boats, some with waders, some on shore, just happy to be fishing and enjoying the sunshine. Further downstream is the Holyoke Generating Station to the west. The area around the station is strewn with powerlines and many times cormorants set themselves atop these wires, apparent masters of all they survey. The Boston & Maine Railroad bridge and the

Boating Facilities and Services	Parking •	Permit Required ☆	Car-Topped Boat Access •	Ramp: Improved/Unimproved	Picnic Area/Water/Rest Rooms/Telephone	Gas/Diesel Fuel	Rent: Fishing Boats/Canoes/Kayaks	Supplies/Food/Bait/Ice	Repairs: Engines/Hulls/Propellers	MasterCard/VISA/American Express
1 Holyoke Dam Access Area North Chicopee Street	•		•	U						
2 Jones Ferry Marina Jones Ferry Road (413) 532-6185	•	☆	•	I	PW RT	G		SF I	E	M V
3 Rte. 90 Ramp Granger Street	•		•	I						
4 Bassett's Marina North End Bridge (413) 739-4745								S	E	M V
5 Riverfront Park Springfield, MA	•		•		PR T					
6 West Springfield Town Ramp Rte. 5	•		•	I						
7* Springfield Yacht Club	PRIVATE CLUB									
8 Pioneer Valley Yacht Club	PRIVATE CLUB									
9 Riverside Park Rte. 159 (413) 786-9300	AMUSEMENT PARK									
10 Thompsonville Town Ramp Asatuck Street	•		•	I						

Information in these listings is provided by the facilities themselves. An asterisk (*) indicates that the facility did not respond to our most recent requests for information.

adjacent **Williamansett Bridge,** (Rte. 141), between Holyoke and Chicopee extend across the River at mile 79.5.

Below the Rte. 391 bridge, Jones Ferry Marina is on the western shore. Complete with restaurant and picnic area, you may want to stop here for a bite to eat. The **Massachusetts Turnpike Bridge,** Rte. 90, is at mile 76. Immediately below the bridge is an access ramp. The launch area has ample parking and can be reached by Granger Street off Rte. 116 in Chicopee. The improved but still badly polluted **Chicopee River** enters 1/2 mile south, right next to an old abandoned hydroelectric plant.

A PLANNED INDUSTRIAL CITY

Holyoke has the distinction of being the first planned industrial community in the United States. It grew from a tranquil hamlet in the 1760s to the "paper city of the world" by the 1880s – with a population of 60,000.

In the 2 miles between Holyoke and South Hadley, the Connecticut River drops 60 feet. It was this natural feature of the River that, in 1846, attracted investors from the eastern part of the state. Recognizing the potential for water-power development, they organized as the Hadley Falls Company and acquired 1,100 acres of land on which they planned a new city, the foundations of which were a great dam and a system of canals.

An immense undertaking for its day, it attracted nationwide attention, and many manufacturing companies and waves of immigrant workers moved to the area. The plan provided areas not only for the mills but also for residences, stores, utilities, churches, a reservoir, parklands, and more. The 4-mile canal was laid out at three different elevations, permitting the water to be used several times over. The first dam had inherent design problems and collapsed on the day of its dedication but was rebuilt the following year in 1849.

A colorful account of the happenings of the day of the first dam's dedication was sent over the newly invented telegraph to the dam's investors in Boston:

10:00 A.M.	Gates just closed; water filling behind dam.
12:00 Noon	Dam leaking badly.
2:00 P.M.	Stones of bulkhead giving way to pressure.
3:20 P.M.	Your old dam's gone to hell by way of Williamansett.

The second Holyoke Dam lasted until 1900 when it was supplanted by the present 1,020-foot granite dam.

Textiles were Holyoke's earliest products, but were soon surpassed by paper. Holyoke continues today as one of the state's largest industrial cities, with a great diversity of products, textiles and paper included. For a truly interesting presentation of the story of Holyoke – complete with graphics and a guide/interpreter – a visit to Holyoke Heritage Park is recommended. ✦

Surprisingly, the confluence of the Chicopee is a good spot for fishing, so you may want to drop a line. The **Rte. I-91 bridge**, adorned in the usual interstate bridge gray and green, crosses the Connecticut at mile 74.5.

Moving south into Springfield, the banks of the River become more residential. The beautiful granite **North End Bridge** comes into view at mile 72.5. Bassett's Marina is on the east bank just below the bridge, as is the WMAS radio tower. The Conrail bridge follows, and then the picturesque **Hampden County Memorial Bridge**. To the east lies the hotel and bank skyline of Springfield.

Springfield's **Riverfront Park** and the nearby Basketball Hall of Fame (413) 781-6500 is at mile 71. The park has a floating dock, so you may want to tie up and take in a bit of hoops history. Slightly south, on the western shore is the West Springfield Town Ramp. The ramp is easily accessible by car via Rte. 5 and has plenty of parking. Less than a mile below this, the **Westfield River** flows in from the west and the **Mill River** from the east. This section of the River has a certain odiferous quality due to a sewage treatment plant at the mouth of the Westfield. The **South End Bridge,** the last of Springfield's bridges, stretches across the Connecticut at mile 70, followed quickly by Springfield Yacht Club.

Below Springfield, the River begins to take on an agricultural air, with pastures and fields lining its banks. The ferris wheel and roller coaster of **Riverside Park** (413) 786-9300 are visible above the trees to the southwest. As you near the amusement park the screams of its riders are often audible. There is good birding at **Willy's Island** near the Massachusetts/Connecticut border and also in the cutback above **Raspberry Brook.** Great blue herons, northern orioles, yellow warblers, and kingfishers populate this area, as do turtles who enjoy sunning themselves in the afternoon. Two miles below the state border, by the old mill town of Thompsonville, you will come to the derelict piers of the old **Rte. 190 bridge,** the truss span was dismantled in 1971. Below the abutments is a town ramp accessible by car via Asatuck Street in Thompsonville.

Three-quarters of a mile farther down is the new **Rte. 190 bridge** and beyond that **Enfield Dam.** Take heed of the warning signs. Though the dam is breached in several locations, running it is not recommended. The dam is nine feet high and is skewed downstream to the west, where a canal lock once admitted boats into the **Windsor Locks Canal.** The waters below the dam are a popular shad-fishing area in the spring, though the dam's deterioration has somwhat reduced its ability to impede the shad's upstream migration.

THE ENFIELD RAPIDS AND
THE WINDSOR LOCKS CANAL

Formerly known as Enfield Falls, the town of Windsor Locks stands just below the Enfield Dam at the head of tidewater navigation on the Connecticut River. The town owed its early importance to the River traffic and necessity of transferring cargo from tidewater vessels, carting it around the falls, and reloading it into flatboats for the remainder of the trip upstream. Only small flatboats could be poled up the rapids. All other cargo had to be pulled overland in oxcarts. Portaging around the rapids continued for almost 200 years until 1829, when the canal and locks were built. The 5-1/2 mile-long canal was an important link for 15 or more years, until the advent of the railroads effectively ended the use of steamboats on the upper River. ✦

© *Duffy Schade*

Shad fishing at the Enfield Dam.

THE VALLEY'S FLOOD-CONTROL SYSTEM

Following the 1936 flood, Congress charged the U.S. Army Corps of Engineers to review the flood problem and propose a plan to minimize the potential for flood damage. The Flood Control Act of 1938 approved a flood-control plan consisting of 20 reservoirs and local protection projects (dikes, levees, and floodwalls) at seven major damage centers: Hartford, East Hartford, Springfield, West Springfield, Holyoke, Northampton, and Chicopee. The Flood Control Act of 1941 authorized the construction of large reservoirs in the upstream areas.

By 1970, 16 upstream reservoirs and seven local protection projects had been completed at a cost of $300 million. It is estimated that in a recurrence of the 1936 flood, over 90 percent of the damage would be avoided. Yet the system is not complete. To protect the damage centers from a "Standard Project Flood," the Corps recommended the construction of seven more upstream reservoirs. The "Standard Project Flood" is defined as the flood that can be expected from the worst combination of the various meteorological and hydrological conditions that are reasonably characteristic of the area. A Standard Project Flood would be the worst flood ever to hit the valley.

Today, if a Standard Project Flood were to occur, the dikes in all the above cities except Hartford would be overtopped. Hartford constructed its floodwalls to a height that would hold back the floodwaters even if the seven additional reservoirs were never built. The other six cities assumed that the reservoirs would be built and constructed their local protection works accordingly.

In 1976, *The River's Reach* was published by the New England River Basin Commission. It recommended that the seven additional reservoirs not be constructed, that the six cities raise their local protection, and that the valley's flood plains be managed to keep people away from flood-hazard area. To date, the reservoirs have not been constructed, the dikes have not been raised, and the valley-wide floodplain management program recommended by *The River's Reach* still has not been instituted. ✦

CRWC Activities in Massachusetts

■ The Council continues to be a leader in opposing the diversion of the Connecticut River or its tributaries as a water supply for eastern Massachusetts.

■ The Council has protected wetlands, riverfront lands, islands, and forestlands through its land conservancy programs.

■ The Council is working to clean up pollution from combined sewer overflows along the River and its tributaries.

■ The Council sponsors river-oriented special events and educational programs for the public.

■ The Council is conducting a River Watch program to monitor the water quality of the Connecticut River and its tributaries and to promote environmental education.

■ CRWC participates with tributary watershed groups in the watershed to design and implement comprehensive river and land use planning.

Connecticut

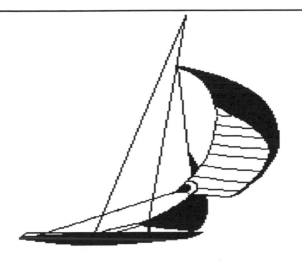

Lynde Point Lighthouse, Old Saybrook, CT.

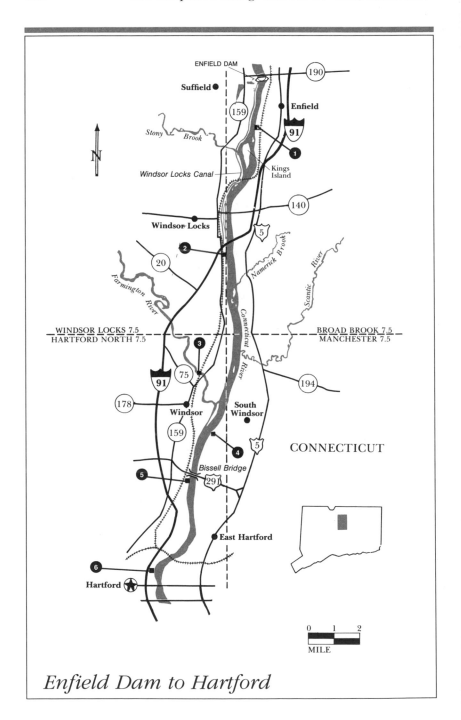

Enfield Dam to Hartford

Enfield Dam to Hartford

MILE FROM MOUTH:	63-49 (14 mile span)
NAVIGABLE BY:	Kayak, canoe, small powerboat, and sailboats near Hartford.
DIFFICULTY:	Class I-II, flat water.
PORTAGES:	None.
CAMPING:	No established sites.
USGS MAPS:	Windsor Locks 7.5. Broad Brook 7.5. Manchester 7.5. Hartford North 7.5.
EMERGENCY HELP:	Enfield 911. Hartford 911.

Between Enfield Dam and Hartford, the Connecticut River has a bit of everything. You'll find rapids and flat water, pastures and cityscapes, marshes and beaches, islands, tributaries, good fishing, birding, and even a few bridges. This region is certainly one of diversity and moderation – if Aristotle had boated here, he would have been pleased.

The area below Enfield Dam is an especially good fishing spot during the shad run in the spring. However, if you're in a canoe or small boat be cautious, the current is extremely quick and the water is shallow. On the west bank is a scenic vista at the beginning of **Windsor Locks Canal,** which at one time was used to ferry boats around Enfield Rapids. Although boats are no longer allowed in the Canal, there is a paved walkway along the Canal which affords a wonderful view of the River.

Swift and shallow water continues as you move south. A mile below the dam is the site of the first bridge in Connecticut across the River. A shelf of ice carried the bridge away in 1898. At mile 61 on the east bank is a well-maintained state access ramp. Slightly downstream of the access ramp are the jagged cliffs of **King's Island.** The island is navigable on either side, though you should watch for shallows near **Stony Brook.**

At mile 60.5, you will pass under the Conrail Bridge. Here, the River will widen slightly, become deeper, and the current will slow down. Also

Boating Facilities and Services	Parking ●	Permit Required ☆	Car-Topped Boat Access	Ramp: Improved/Unimproved	Picnic Area/Water/Rest Rooms/Telephone	Gas/Diesel Fuel	Rent: Fishing Boats/Canoes/Kayaks	Supplies/Food/Bait/Ice	Repairs: Engines/Hulls/Propellers	MasterCard/VISA/American Express
❶ Enfield State Ramp Parsons Road	●		●	I						
❷ Windsor Locks Town Ramp Rte. 159	●		●	I						
❸ Windsor Town Ramp (On Farmington River), Rte. 159	●		●	I	PWT			SF		
❹ South Windsor Town Ramp Old Main Street	●		●	I						
❺ Bissell Bridge Launch East Barbar Street	●		●	I						
❻ Riverside Park I-91 (Exit 33)	●		●	I	P					

Information in these listings is provided by the facilities themselves. An asterisk (*) indicates that the facility did not respond to our most recent requests for information.

from this point on, you will begin to experience tidal fluctuations, which is of particular importance if you venture into any of the coves or inlets further south. A mile below the railroad bridge is the **Rte. 140 bridge** at Windsor Locks, followed a mile later by the **Dexter Coffin Bridge,** Rte. I-91. On the west bank, just before the I-91 bridge are the three lower locks that link the Windsor Locks Canal with the River. There is a public ramp below the Dexter Coffin Bridge on the western shore. The ramp is accessible by car via Route 159.

Ducks frequently travel the River here. Cardinals, robins, swallows, and cormorants can also be found in large numbers and tend to congregate around the sedimentary islands below the Rte. I-91 bridge, which shift over time. At mile 54, the winding and narrow Scantic River flows in from the east. Across to the west, the entrance to the **Farmington River** at mile 53 is obscured by a large island at its mouth. This important tributary is a prime spawning ground for Atlantic salmon and American shad. During the spring the shores along the Farmington are crowded with fishermen. There is an access ramp to the Farmington just upstream of the Rte. 159 bridge and close to Bart's Deli (203) 688-9035, which is a

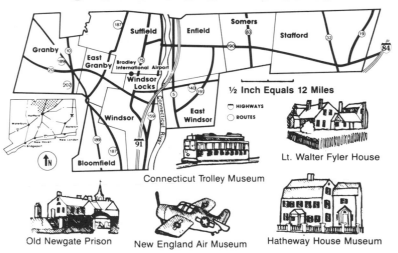

nice spot for lunch. The Farmington also offers some of the best whitewater in southern New England. If you have the time, it is worth a trip up this river. A complete guide to the river can be obtained from the Farmington River Watershed Association, 749 Hopmeadow St., Simsbury, CT 06070, (203) 658-4442.

Below the entrance to the Farmington, on the east bank, is the South Windsor town launch area. There is plenty of parking available and the ramp can be reached via Old Main Street in South Windsor. Continuing downstream, the River grows steadily wider, so winds will be of greater concern to the small boater. In Windsor, under the **Bissell Bridge,** Rte. 291, there is another boat ramp. While you're there, you may want to drop a line since the Bissell bridge is a known hot spot for fishing. There is a railroad bridge at mile 49.5 and from here the skyline of Hartford should be in view. You can take out in Hartford at **Riverside Park,** which is a large open area with ample room for picnics, frisbee, or walking along the riverbank. To get to the park by car take exit 33 off Rte. I-91.

Skyline of Hartford, CT with the Penn Central Railroad Bridge in the foreground.

© Embassy

MARK TWAIN

Samuel Clemens, alias Mark Twain, first visited Hartford in 1868, writing, "Of all the beautiful towns it has been my fortune to see, this is the chief." Five years later, he moved with his wife to a rambling Victorian Gothic house he had built on Farmington Avenue. The first floor was decorated by Louis Comfort Tiffany; the kitchen was in the front of the house so the servants could see the goings-on in the street; and in the back was a room in the shape of a pilot's house. As *The Hartford Courant* noted, "The novelty displayed in the architecture of the building, the oddity of its internal arrangements, and the fame of its owner will all conspire to make it a house of note for a long time to come."

Twain wrote of this house, "To us, our house was not unsentient matter-it had a heart and soul...It was us, and we were its confidence, and lived in the grace and the peace of its benediction. We never came home from an absence that its face did not light up and speak its eloquent welcome – and we could not enter it unmoved."

Adjacent to the Twain house is the home of Harriet Beecher Stowe, the author of *Uncle Tom's Cabin*. Both houses are now part of the Nook Farm Complex and are open to the public. Call (203) 525-9317 for additional information. ◆

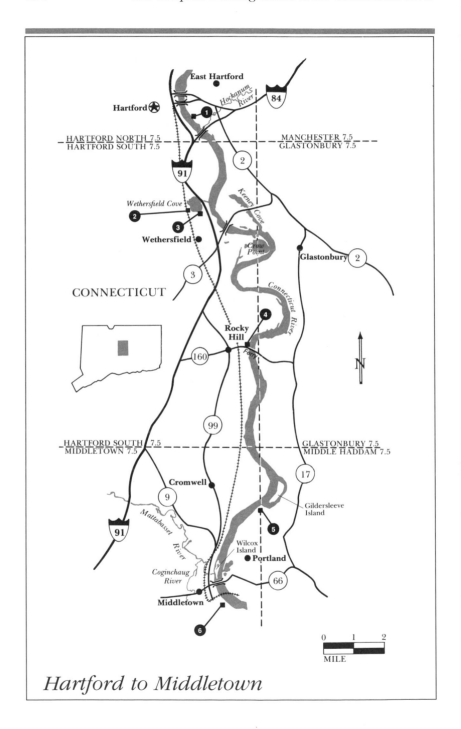

Hartford to Middletown

Hartford to Middletown

MILE FROM MOUTH:	49-30 (19 mile span).
NAVIGABLE BY:	All craft with drafts less than 15' and mast heights less than 81' (below mile 47.5).
DIFFICULTY:	Flat water. Beware of tides, winds, and boat wakes.
PORTAGES:	None.
CAMPING:	No established sites.
USGS MAPS:	Hartford North, 7.5. Hartford South 7.5. Glastonbury 7.5. Middletown 7.5. Middle Haddam 7.5.
NOAA CHARTS:	Connecticut River:Bodkin Rock to Hartford (#12377).
EMERGENCY HELP:	911.

Hartford's skyline is beautiful, especially when viewed from a boat on the Connecticut River. The City's main access to the River is at **Riverside Park,** on the west bank about 1/2 mile above the three highway bridges, where there is a ramp. Beneath the Morgan Bulkeley Bridge, you will notice that the span closest to Hartford is metal, while the others are stone; this was done to facilitate the inclusion of a draw if it were ever needed.

The **Park River** enters the Connecticut between the **Founders** and **Charter Oak** bridges but cannot be seen as the city covered it over because of heavy pollution. There is a sewage treatment plant west of Brainerd Field, and the city is now building a new treatment facility for combined sewer overflow. Still, Hartford sewers can contaminate up to 16-miles of the River after heavy rains.

Across from the bridges is the dock for the *Lady Fenwick* (203) 526-4954 – a small excursion boat offering afternoon and evening trips on the River heading either north to Windsor or south to Middletown.

Boating Facilities and Services	Parking • / Permit Required ☆	Car-Topped Boat Access	Ramp: Improved/Unimproved	Picnic Area/Water/Rest Rooms/Telephone	Gas/Diesel Fuel	Rent: Fishing Boats/Canoes/Kayaks	Supplies/Food/Bait/Ice	Repairs: Engines/Hulls/Propellers	MasterCard/VISA/American Express
1 State Boat Ramp, Great River Park, East River Drive	• ☆	•	I	P R					
2 Wethersfield Cove Yacht Club, Wethersfield, CT (203) 563-8780	PRIVATE CLUB								
3 Wethersfield Cove Ramp, River Road	• ☆	•	I	P R					
4 Rocky Hill Ferry & Ramp, Glastonbury Avenue	• ☆	•	I	P R					
5 Petzold's Marine Center, Off Rte. 17A (203) 342-1196	•			WR T	G		S	EH P	M V
6 Harbor Park, Off Rte. 91				•					

Information in these listings is provided by the facilities themselves. An asterisk (*) indicates that the facility did not respond to our most recent requests for information.

In **East Hartford,** below the Founders Bridge, you'll find a town boat ramp, which may be reached by crossing the River on Rte. 84 and then taking the River Rd. exit into East Hartford. The ramp is located off East River Drive. When launching a small boat, beware that the current runs at a good clip – you may be well downstream before the motor starts.

Over the years, Hartford has been home to a number of well-known people, Mark Twain, Harriet Beecher Stowe, and Wallace Stevens among them. You may want to head into the city to see the attractions. If you do, we suggest you lock up your boat – providing it's not large – at the small dock at the boat ramp in East Hartford and then cross the bridges by foot.

Below the **Charter Oak Bridge,** a channel 15 feet deep and 150 feet wide is maintained by the Army Corps of Engineers. Coastal tankers and oil barges often come as far north as Hartford, and as neither vessel has great maneuverability, all other boats must yield to their right of way. You must also be cautious of heavy wakes, thrown both by ships and large pleasure craft. These wakes can capsize even the most skilled canoeists. Large boats must remember to slow down when near a canoe or other small boats – it is both common courtesy and the law – and small boaters must stay out of the main channels.

Continuing south below Hartford, you'll see the entrance to **Wethersfield Cove** cutting into the west bank at about mile 45. The narrow inlet leading to the cove is usually marked with privately maintained aids, and is cut off from the River by a bridge with a vertical height of only about 25 feet. Once you enter the cove, you will see a ramp on the southeast shore. There is plenty of parking, but the grade leading into the water is gradual, making it difficult to launch a boat. In fact, just pulling ashore can be a trick, especially if the wind is running from behind. It's easy to get the bow of the boat close to shore, but not quite close enough so you can jump without getting wet.

Wethersfield Cove Yacht Club, on the south-western shore, maintains a fair number of moorings in the cove, so keep an eye out if you're running with a prop. The northern shores of the cove are part of **Folly Brook Preserve,** a 20-30 acre nature sanctuary which has been set aside for study of the flood plain habitat. Wethersfield is a pleasant historical village with a number of old houses open to visitors.

Below the cove, you will pass under the Rte. 3 **Putnam Bridge** between Wethersfield and Glastonbury. On the east shore, just above a gas tank farm, **Keeney Cove** cuts back north and passes under the bridge again. The channel is obscured by low-lying trees. On the west bank, as you enter the cove, you'll find a conservation area and bird sanctuary. Upstream, you'll pass by a favorite local fishing spot near the **Point Road Bridge.** The cove was once a River channel and still extends into East Hartford. In spring, when the water is high, a dangerous current often develops at the mouth of the cove and then again beneath the highway bridge, so be cautious when entering.

Crow Point and the **Crow Point Basin** follow on the west bank as the River bends south. The basin was created by dredging for fill used in the construction of I-91. The basin runs about 4 feet deep and has a good bottom for dropping anchor, but getting in sometimes poses a problem.

Before reaching **Rocky Hill,** you will drift along a stretch of River with industrial decoration. There are gas and oil tank farms dotting the banks. You will also pass some attractive scenery and a few sandy beaches that are fine for picnics, as long as you keep an eye out for poison ivy.

After passing a condominium complex on the east bank in Glastonbury, watch for the outflow of **Meadow Brook.** There is a space for small craft to tie-up for a visit to the **Connecticut Audubon Holland Brook Center** (203) 633-8402 next to the town's **Earle Park Preserve.**

The ferry running from Rocky Hill to Glastonbury is the oldest ferry in the country, having begun in 1655. Today, it is run by a small tug, but at various times throughout its history, the ferry was driven by wooden poles, oars, a horse-powered treadmill, and a steam engine. Crossing time is now 4 minutes, with a cost of $1.00 per car and 25 cents for each additional passenger. The ferry carries 3 to 4 cars maximum, and though it doesn't run on a fixed schedule, it can be hailed with a honk of the horn. There is a fine launching ramp next to the ferry landing in Rocky Hill, but none in Glastonbury. It's about a mile or so into Rocky Hill proper, and another few miles from there to reach Dinosaur State Park (203) 529-8423. (See the sidebar in this chapter for more information on the park.)

For the next 8 miles, the River is quite straight and passes through hilly, wooded countryside. On the west shore, just above daybeacon J, you will see a small tributary that winds deep into the woods and brings you to an eerie, lost land of pale green ferns and flooded banks with trees dipping toward the water. There is a large tree crossing the water about 1/4 mile along. Canoeists can continue from here for a fair bit.

Continuing south, you will pass **Gildersleeve Island.** Small boats may want to leave the main channel and pass west of the island, both to escape the traffic and to get out of the wind. A landing on the east bank of the River sits directly opposite the island and can be reached via Rte. 17A in Portland. Just below the island is **Petzold's Marine Center,** a large marina with all the facilities even the larger pleasure boats will need.

DANGER: A submerged dike runs across the northern end of Gildersleeve Island's western side. The dike was built to direct water to the east side of the island and to keep the main channel open. Also, the River is affected by the tide this far south, so keep an eye on the changes, which can be found in local newspapers, at the marinas, or in a number of tide guides.

Well south of Gildersleeve, to the east side of the River, is **Wilcox Island** [29.5]. Just above Wilcox a large storm drain should be avoided. There are orange and white markers which will keep you away from the powerful surge of water. Wilcox Island can easily be seen from Rte. 91. Passing the island, large boats should stick to the east channel. Small boats may want to head down the western passage, which is less congested during the summer. Just beware of the rocky shallows at the head of the island.

The **Mattabasset River** meets the Connecticut about 3/4 of the way along Wilcox Island. At the River's mouth is a ramp owned by the Cromwell Outboard Private Association which can't be used without permission. Entering the Mattabasset, you will pass below the Rte. 9 bridge and the railroad bridge. Rounding your first turn, a car is lying on the bank, decaying. Soon, you will encounter the aroma of a landfill.

Municipalities place their landfills next to rivers so that there is no question of where the run-off will end up. The landfills are built near marshland, which is primary to the natural food chain, because it is devalued and easy to manipulate. If you can stand the smell, and it gets worse in the heat of summer, the Mattabasset is a nice side trip, running

Rocky Hill-Glastonbury ferry.

about 2 miles. Once beyond the landfill, which has spread around varied articles of plastic and paper, the river opens into a wide marshland that provides home to many animals, particularly ducks and hawks.

Back on the Connecticut, the **Arrigoni Bridge** brings cars from Middletown to Portland. Just below the Arrigoni is the old railroad bridge, which was destroyed in 1876 when the steamship *The City of Hartford* accidentally rammed the bridge and one of the pilings. Apparently, the pilot had somehow mistaken the bridge lights for the lights on shore. From that time on, all bridges across the country wore red and green lights, rather than the white lights that had been used previously.

Another 1/2 mile will bring you to **Middletown's Harbor Park** and the **America's Cup Restaurant,** where there is a dock and an outdoor lounge. Next to the restaurant is the **Wesleyan University Boat House,** where the rowing shells are kept. The Head of the Connecticut Regatta is held here every fall. Middletown itself is about three blocks away, across Rte. 9 and up the hill. You should be able to find anything you want along Main Street, all within a short walk of the River. The town of Portland is also within easy walking distance of the River. There are no docks on that side, but you can tie up at one of the marinas for a small fee.

CONNECTICUT RIVER STEAMBOATS

Essex's Steamboat Dock, now the Connecticut River Museum, and Goodspeed's Landing in East Haddam are two of the few remaining landings left from the days when the great steamboats ran the Connecticut River. Regular service from Hartford to New York, and places in between, began in 1822 and lasted until 1931. At first small and awkward, the steamboats grew in size, speed, and luxuriousness, becoming floating palaces bedecked with velvet and crystal. One of the last of the fleet, the *Middletown,* was 243 feet long, 145 feet wide, with 1,554 gross tonnage. It had accommodations for 350 passengers. The steamboats formed an important link for the River towns and the large metropolitan areas of New York and Boston. The smooth ride of a steamboat was also much preferred to the bouncy and slow stage coaches.

These beautiful boats also had their share of troubles. The *Ellsworth's* boiler exploded off Essex in 1827, as did the *New England's* in 1933. The *City of Hartford* hit both the Lyme and Middletown railroad bridges. The *State of New York* caught fire at East Haddam in 1881, followed by the *Granite State* at the same location two years later. The best of the steamboat years were from 1892 to 1917. Thereafter, competition from the railroads and the automobile sealed their doom. The last steamboat trip on the River was made by the *Hartford* on October 31, 1931.　✦

© Connecticut River Foundation

The steamship, City of Hartford *collided with the Middletown railroad bridge, March 29, 1876.*

Drop anchor in the lower Connecticut River Valley. Join us in the sights and sounds of our river and shoreline towns.

Call or write for free information:

Connecticut Valley Tourism Commission

393 Main Street
Middletown, CT 06457

(203) 347-6924

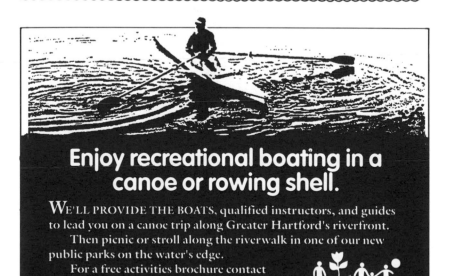

DINOSAURS

In 1802, Pliny Moody was plowing his field in South Hadley, MA when he came across what seemed to be giant bird foot prints in a piece of brownstone. Moody was intrigued enough to use the stone as his front doorstep. Although he didn't know it, Moody had found the first fossil evidence of dinosaurs in the New World. In 1818, the fossilized bones of a 6-foot-tall bird were unearthed in East Windsor, CT.

While the tracks and bones themselves were not very impressive, the evidence of extinct species had profound implications. No longer could the Bible be interpreted literally, because these rocks were much older than any date given in the religious texts, and were made up of rocks even older than that. Within a generation, the accepted age of the earth went from roughly 6,000 years to nearly 4.6 billion years.

Other dinosaur tracks were found in the soft sedimentary mud that later cemented into brownstone throughout the central valley of the Connecticut River. Perhaps the best, and certainly the best-preserved, dinosaur tracks were found in Rocky Hill, CT by an alert bulldozer operator who was working on a state building site in 1966. Five hundred of the 2,000 in situ tracks can be seen at Dinosaur State Park (203) 529-8423, enclosed in a 40-foot-high geodesic dome. There is a boardwalk over the tracks so that visitors can get a close view of the footprints left in stone by the Dilophosaurus, or "Double-crested Lizard," about 185 million years ago. There is a casting area at the park where, if you bring your own plaster, you can make casts of the giant footprints. This area is open from May through October, during the day.   ✦

CRWC Activities in Connecticut

- The Council has protected hundreds of acres of wetlands, riverfront lands, and forest lands through its Land Conservancy program.

- The Council co-founded the Connecticut Clean Water Coalition.

- The Council is working to ensure long-term funding for municipal sewage projects in an effort to reduce the Combined Sewer Overflow pollution to the river.

- CRWC works with towns in Connecticut to inventory natural, historical, and cultural resources and to design and implement action plans and comprehensive river and land-use planning.

- The Council's River Watch Program in Connecticut includes a hotline where local volunteers can report possible problems spotted in or near the River.

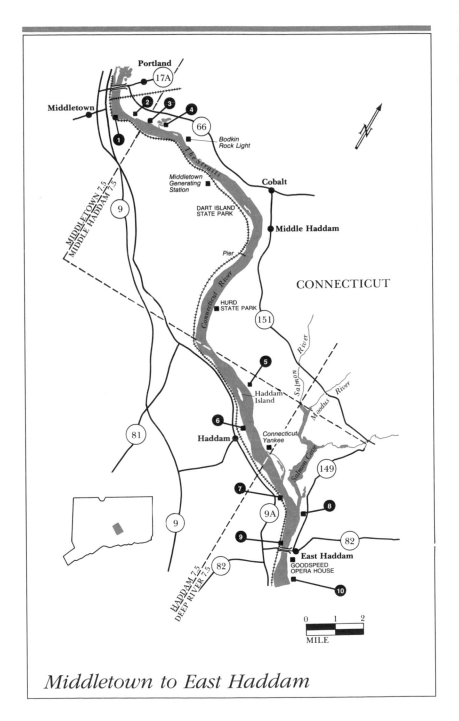

Middletown to East Haddam

Middletown to East Haddam

MILE FROM MOUTH:	30.5-15.0 (15.5 mile span).
NAVIGABLE BY:	All craft drawing less than 15' with mast heights less than 81'.
DIFFICULTY:	Flat water. Beware of tides, wind, and boat wakes.
PORTAGES:	None.
CAMPING:	Mile 23.0, Hurd State Park, Haddam Neck, CT (203) 526-2336.
USGS MAPS:	Middletown 7.5. Middle Haddam 7.5. Haddam 7.5. Deep River 7.5.
NOAA CHARTS:	Connecticut River: Bodkin Rock to Hartford (#12377); Deep River to Bodkin Rock (#12377).
RECOMMENDED:	Tidal Currents Tables: Atlantic Coast of North America (Dept. of Commerce) or Eldridge Tide and Coast Pilot.
EMERGENCY HELP:	911.

Heading downstream from Middletown, you soon notice changes in the River. The shallow channel flowing through a wide floodplain now runs deeper and passes between old hills of metamorphic rock, schists, gneiss, and pegmatite. The River is generally deeper and straighter, and the green plains of fern that decorated the muddy banks above have become high, ledgy cliffs topped with mixed forests of maple, oak, and hemlock.

You may be able to carry a canoe or kayak to the water at **Middletown's Harbor Park,** where you'll find the **America's Cup Restaurant.** Boats that require a ramp have to be put in across the River in Portland, where there are several marinas that will charge you for the service. Next door to America's Cup you will see the **Wesleyan**

Boating Facilities and Services

	Parking ● / Permit Required ☆	Car-Topped Boat Access	Ramp: Improved/Unimproved	Picnic Area/Water/Rest Rooms/Telephone	Gas/Diesel Fuel	Rent: Fishing Boats/Canoes/Kayaks	Supplies/Food/Bait/Ice	Repairs: Engines/Hulls/Propellers	MasterCard/VISA/American Express
1 Harbor Park, Off Rte. 91		●							
2 Crowley & Holmes Riverside Marina, Riverview Street (203) 342-1911	●			P R T			S I	E H P	M V
3 Yankee Boat Yard Marina, Riverview Street (203) 342-4735	● ☆	●	I	P W R T	G		B I	E H P	M V
4 Portland Boat Works, Grove Street (203) 342-1085					G		S	E H	M V
5 Rock Landing, Rock Landing Road		●	U						
6 Haddam Meadows State Park, Off Rte. 154	●	●	I	P R					
7 Midway Marina, Rte. 154 (203) 345-4330	● ☆		I	W R			S I	E H P	M V
8 Salmon River State Ramp, Rte. 149	●	●	I						
9 Andrew's Marina, Bridge Road (203) 345-2286					G		I		M V
10 East Haddam Access, Lumber Yard Road		●							

Information in these listings is provided by the facilities themselves. An asterisk (*) indicates that the facility did not respond to our most recent requests for information.

Boathouse, where the crew team begins and ends its daily workouts. Keep an eye out for these delicate rowing shells while you're on the River – even the slightest wake can swamp them or will at least cause an oarsman to catch a crab, which is nearly as bad. Remember, you are responsible for any damage caused by your wake.

Portland, the cross-River sister of Middletown, was once site of the quarries that supplied stone for New York's famous brownstones. You will see litter dotting the shores of both cities, some of it just reckless and some more substantial. As you leave the cities behind, you will pass the WCNX broadcast tower on the west bank, and just below that, one of the towers housing the Telemark advanced flood warning system.

On the west side of the River, directly across from Portland Boat Works is a small municipal park with a good boat ramp, which can be reached by way of River Road. A few hundred yards further brings you to **Bodkin Rock** and the **Straits.** You can see some fine examples of folded metamorphic rock along the banks, and on the west shore you will pass a feldspar mine and processing plant.

Also on the west shore, about a half-mile below the mine, is the **Middletown Power Station** (203) 346-9639, operated by Northeast Utilities. This small, oil-fired electric plant cannot be reached from the water. There is often heavy barge traffic in front of the plant, so stay to the east shore. Power boats should also beware of shallow spots running along the west shore, which are often no more than 2 feet deep at low tide; look for sea gulls that seem to be standing on water.

At mile 24.5, you will pass **Dart Island** on the River's west side. The island is an undeveloped State Park with limited access. No camping is allowed. Over the years, Dart Island has varied in nature from island to peninsula many times, so beware of heading along the inner passage as the water may be shallow or even gone, depending on the season. Across the River, a sandy beach may serve as a landing for those wishing to head in to the village of **Middle Haddam.** Mostly old houses and quiet neighbors, the town is more appealing than exciting. Also look for the nearby cobalt mine, which has been exploited intermittently since 1762 in the never-finished quest for cobalt, mica, and nickel. In 1987, the University of Connecticut raised a few eyebrows when they discovered trace amounts of gold in the mine. You may want to try a little panning for gold in the quiet shallows of **Mine Brook.**

Throughout colonial times and well into the 19th century, shipbuilding flourished in the many River towns, including Middle Haddam. Lumber came from the local oak and hemlock trees, as well as the occasional logs which floated by from upstream. More than 4,000 ships were built, many for trans-Atlantic crossings.

About a mile below Dart Island, a sewage treatment plant pier juts out from the west bank; and just below it, another pier extends well into the River, this one belonging to Pratt & Whitney, which owns an amazing amount of land along the River. This plant caused a lot of noise pollution – testing different turbines for jet engines – until local residents forced the company to install noise filters throughout the facility.

Another mile along, on the east bank, is **Hurd State Park.** There are many good trails for hiking and spots for camping in the park, and there is a fine beach – the water from here to the Sound is Class B, suitable for fishing or swimming. The park can be recognized by a breakwater which runs the length of its waterfront. **The Connecticut River Raft Race –** which is a zany conglomeration of people-powered, home-made, floating, water-vessels – begins at the Park and then winds its way down to **Haddam Meadows State Park** about five miles below. Scores of floaters, on rafts of all shapes and sizes, make the voyage downriver each summer in hopes of a good time, as well as gaining distinction as the best River floaters around. Haddam Meadows is also the site of the Quinnehtukqut Rendezvous and Native American Festival (203) 347-6924 held on the third weekend in August. The festival includes dance competitions, a demonstration village, colonial crafts, and a black-powder musket shoot.

South of the park, at about mile 20, is **Haddam Island State Park,** with a sand beach for landing and sunbathing. The island is a good destination for a day trip as it offers a picnic spot and swimming, but camping is not allowed. On the east shore near the tip of the island, you will also see Rock Landing with an unimproved ramp and isolated access.

At this spot, high-tension power cables run across the River from the **Connecticut Yankee Atomic Power Company** (203) 267-9279. The plant is one of the nation's oldest and once set a world record for most days in continuous operation. Visitors are welcome to tie up at a dock outside the plant, and tours of the facility are available to those who call ahead. The Energy Information Center offers visitors literature discussing specifics of nuclear power production and also provides nature trails in the surrounding countryside. You can pick up guidebooks at the Information Center that will show you through open plains and across rocky ledges and will suggest interesting activities along the way.

Below the plant, on the east side of the River is Connecticut Yankee's cooling water discharge canal. A set of small booms keep boats from this canal, but fishermen are welcome to wet a line in anticipation of snagging one of the many spiny fins attracted to the warm water.

Haddam Meadows State Park is on the west bank, just across from the power plant. There is an excellent cement ramp at the park which is large enough for any trailered boat. You'll also find a picnic area with tables, outdoor toilets, and lots of parking. The large ball field attracts crowds tossing frisbees and softballs. This a good place to look for hawks and swallows, though the birding isn't nearly what it was even a few years ago. The Meadows are the ending point for the annual Connecticut River Raft Race. The park may be reached by way of Rte. 154.

Below Haddam Meadows and the power plant, power boats should stick to the marked channel, as it is very shallow outside the buoys and you may bend a prop or get hung up in soft stuff.

Salmon Cove and the **Salmon River** open on the east bank about 16.5 miles north of the River mouth. A large, well-maintained state ramp marks the cove entrance. The marshes and backwaters of the cove and along the river are rich with birds and other wildlife. You can proceed upstream about 4 miles to the fish ladder at the **Leesville Dam** in a

THE GOODSPEED OPERA HOUSE

Built in 1876, the Goodspeed Opera House is a fine example of Victorian architecture. Lavishly decorated and a tad eccentric, it not only held a 400-seat theater and a bar, but also a post office, a dry-goods store, and a freight warehouse. William Goodspeed – builder, owner, and namesake – planned things well for the passengers on his steamships, which traveled both to Hartford and New York. While the steamship was being loaded or unloaded, passengers could either watch a Broadway production at his theater or toss a few back at the bar. And if they wanted, they could head next door to his restaurant for a bite to eat.

After falling into disrepair in the 1900s, the opera house was threatened by the wrecking ball in 1963. In an eleventh hour desperation effort, the building was bought from the state by a non-profit preservation group – for one dollar. After extensive reconstruction, the opera house is now the nation's premier theater for American musical comedy. The Broadway hits *Man of La Mancha, Annie,* and *Shenandoah* were premiered at the Goodspeed. Tours of theater, as well as production tickets, are available by calling the box office (203) 873-8668. ✦

© *Connecticut River Watershed Council/Nacul Center*

shallow draft boat. The channel through Salmon Cove is narrow and windy, however, so be cautious. Pay particular attention to the tides, as much of the cove is only about a foot deep at low tide. Above the dam, the upper Salmon is great for whitewater boating and fishing during spring and fall and tubing during the summer.

A mile below the Salmon, at mile 15.5, is the **Rte. 82 Bridge** in **East Haddam.** This is one of the oldest turnstile bridges in the country. For more information about East Haddam, which is home to both the **Goodspeed Opera House** and the **Nathan Hale School House,** see the following chapter covering East Haddam to Essex. You may tie up at **Goodspeed's Landing** or at the town dock, just below, for short periods. If you'd like to stay longer, head to **Andrew's Marina** across the River. There is a small, unimproved access just below the opera house where you can put in a canoe or kayak. The ramp at the airport, which is much wider and would be useful to launch trailered boats, is for seaplanes and can only be used with permission.

© *Duffy Schade*

Gillette Castle.

GILLETTE CASTLE

What looks like an old castle sitting high on a hill overlooking the Connecticut River was once the home of the actor William Gillette and is now Gillette Castle State Park. A native son of Connecticut, Gillette traveled to New York where he immortalized himself portraying Sherlock Holmes. Taking time off from the stage, Gillette took a leisurely cruise up the Connecticut River in 1913. He found the area so enchanting that he gave up his plans to build a house on Long Island and instead bought 122 acres in Hadlyme, CT. After five years and a million dollars, Gillette had finished his castle atop a hill known as "The Seventh Sister."

Every detail inside the castle was from Gillette's own design: the 4-foot-thick stone walls, the hand-carved oak doors, the light switches, even the serpentine driveway from the ferry landing. However, Gillette's pride and joy was his private railroad – two steam engines ran throughout the property over ornate bridges, through a tunnel, and along the edge of the River. Gillette's other hobbies included caring for 15 cats, a variety of goldfish, and two pet frogs that he kept in the pool in the conservatory.

Before he died in 1937, Gillette directed his executors "to see that the property did not fall into the hands of some blithering saphead who has no conception of where he is or with what surrounded." Faithful to his wishes, his executors saw that the Castle became a state park in 1943. The trains and track have since been dismantled, but many of the elegant bridges are still part of the park's trails. Exploring the castle and the grounds is a great way to spend a few hours, especially if the weather is good, since the view of the Connecticut is splendid.

The Park is open Monday – Sunday, 8:00 a.m. to sunset. The Castle is open from Memorial Day – Columbus Day, 10:00 a.m. to 5:00 p.m. on weekdays and 10:00 a.m. to 4:00 p.m. on weekends. For more information call the park manager at (203) 526-2336. ✦

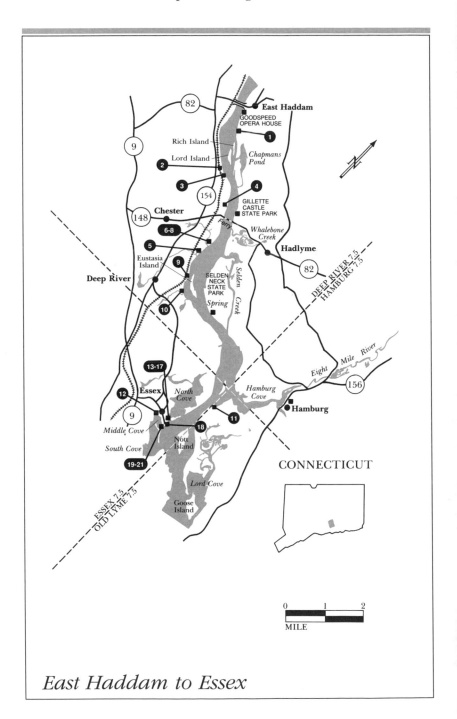

East Haddam to Essex

East Haddam to Essex

MILE FROM MOUTH:	15.5-6.0 (9.5 mile span).
NAVIGABLE BY:	All craft with drafts less than 15' and mast heights less than 81'.
DIFFICULTY:	Flat water. (Beware of tides, winds, and boat wakes).
PORTAGES:	None.
CAMPING:	Mile 12.5, Gillette Castle State Park, Hadlyme, CT, (203) 526-2336.
	Mile 11.5, Selden Neck State Park, Hadlyme, CT (203) 526-2336.
USGS MAPS:	Deep River 7.5. Hamburg 7.5. Essex 7.5. Old Lyme 7.5.
NOAA CHARTS:	Connecticut River: Deep River to Bodkin Rock (#12377). Long Island Sound to Deep River (#12375).
RECOMMENDED:	Tidal Currents Tables; Atlantic Coast of North America (Dept. of Commerce) or Eldridge Tide and Coast Pilot.
EMERGENCY HELP:	East Haddam 911, VHF 16

The area between East Haddam and Essex is one of the most beautiful stretches of the Connecticut River. Subject to development restrictions overseen by the Connecticut River Gateway Commission, the jagged and lofty shores blossom with oaks, elms, aspens, pines, and a host of other species of trees indigenous to the Lower Valley. Only occasionally is the foliage of the rocky banks interrupted by a house or building. The careful observer is certain to spot numerous birds and other riverside wildlife

Boating Facilities and Services

	Parking ● / Permit Required ☆	Car-Topped Boat Access	Ramp: Improved/Unimproved	Picnic Area/Water/Rest Rooms/Telephone	Gas/Diesel Fuel	Supplies/Food/Bait/Ice	Rent: Fishing Boats/Canoes/Kayaks	Repairs: Engines/Hulls/Propellers	MasterCard/VISA/American Express
1 East Haddam Access Area Lumber Yard Road		●							
2 Middletown Yacht Club Rte. 154 (203) 526-5634									
3 Chester Town Ramp Parkers Point Road	●	●	I						
4 Chrisholm Marina Rte. 154 (203) 526-5147					G/D	S/I			M/V
5 Pattaconic Yacht Club Door Road (203) 526-5626						S/I			M/V
6 Hays Haven Marina Railroad Avenue (203) 526-9366					G/D	S/I			M/V
7 Chester Marina Railroad Avenue (203) 526-2227						S/I		P	M/V
8 Connecticut River Marina Railroad Avenue (203) 526-9076						SI/F			
9 Deep River Town Landing River Road	●	●	I						
10 Deep River Marina River Street (203) 526-5560					G/D	S/I		H	M/V
11 Lyme Town Access Area Ely Road	●	●							
12 Middle Cove Marina Middle Cove (203) 767-2641				WR/T					
13 Essex Boat Works Ferry Street (203) 767-8276									M/V
14 Essex Boat House Dauntless Shipyard (203) 767-1781						S			MV/A
15 Embassy Marine Publishing 37 Pratt Street (203) 767-1343	PUBLISHER OF EMBASSY BOATING GUIDES								MV/A
16 Brewer's Dauntless Shipyard Dauntless Shipyard (203) 767-2483				W/T				I	M/V

Boating Facilities and Services		Parking ●	Permit Required ☆	Car-Topped Boat Access	Ramp: Improved/Unimproved	Picnic Area/Water/Rest Rooms/Telephone	Gas/Diesel Fuel	Supplies/Food/Bait/Ice	Rent: Fishing Boats/Canoes/Kayaks	Repairs: Engines/Hulls/Propellers	MasterCard/VISA/American Express
⑰ Essex Island Marina Essex Island (203) 767-1267						WR T	G D	SF I			MV A
⑱ Essex Town Ramp Foot of Main Street		●			I	P					
⑲ Essex Yacht Club Novelty Lane (203) 767-8121						PRIVATE CLUB					
⑳ Essex Corinthian Yacht Club Novelty Lane (203) 767-3239						PRIVATE CLUB					
㉑ Brewer's Chandlery East Novelty Lane (203) 767-8267						W T	G D	S I			MV A

Information in these listings is provided by the facilities themselves. An asterisk (*) indicates that the facility did not respond to our most recent requests for information.

since the entire region is brimming with heron, ducks, kildeer, swans, foxes, muskrat, and many other animals. In addition, the numerous creeks and coves that dot the landscape make terrific side trips away from the noise, bustle, and large wakes of the main channel.

The **East Haddam Bridge,** which is one of the largest and oldest turnstile bridges in the country, has a vertical clearance of 24 feet at mean low water when closed. If this will not allow you to pass, blow your horn three times, or call the bridge operator on VHF channel 13. There is considerable traffic across the bridge between East Haddam and the western shore, so don't be surprised if the bridge operator waits until there are several boats needing to pass before opening.

If you find yourself with the time, the town of East Haddam is well worth a visit – there aren't too many places like it. The **Goodspeed Opera House** (203) 873-8668, which stands prominently on the eastern shore, is an impressive 400-seat theater where you can take in both a Broadway musical and a spectacular view of the River. On the hilltop just upstream of the opera house is the **Nathan Hale Schoolhouse** where the patriot Nathan Hale taught youngsters in a one-room structure during the winter of 1773-74. Right next door is **St. Stephen's Episcopal Church,** the steeple of which houses a bell cast in 815 A.D., purportedly the oldest bell

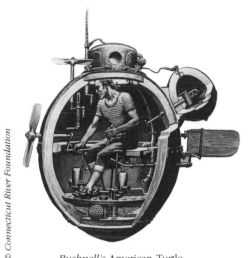

Bushnell's American Turtle.

DAVID BUSHNELL
AND *THE AMERICAN TURTLE*

It is fitting, although only a coincidence, that the nation's submarine fleet is based in the home state of the submarine's inventor: David Bushnell of Westbrook, CT. Born in 1740, Bushnell entered Yale at the age of 31. During his senior year, he astonished classmates and professors by exploding two ounces of gunpowder underwater. At the time of Bushnell's graduation in 1775, hostilities between the American colonies and the British were growing steadily. Bushnell's patriotism led him to apply his knowledge of underwater explosives to the development of underwater mines and a means of getting them to their targets. The result was *The American Turtle*, the first successful submarine.

Bushnell's submarine was named *The American Turtle* because it resembled two tortoise shells bolted together. It was built of oak and steel similar to a large wine cask, and was propelled by means of hand-driven propellers. It could submerge or rise by turning a vertical propeller or by pumping water into or out of the bilge. The operator navigated by the phosphorescent tips of a compass and depth gauge. *The American Turtle* was also outfitted with a sharp steel screw that could be screwed into the bottom of enemy ships. A mine with a timing device was attached to the screw and set to detonate after the submarine had escaped.

Bushnell made the first trial run of *The American Turtle* on the Connecticut River off Ayer's Point. He was then sent by General George Washington to New York Harbor to sink the 64-gun British flagship, the *Eagle*. Unfortunately, the usual operator of the submarine fell sick and had to be replaced by an inexperienced Ezra Lee. Lee managed to get under the *Eagle,* but was unable to attach the mine. As daybreak was coming, he decided to retreat and try again another night. However, his retreat was seen by the British and in order to escape, he set off the mine, keeping the British at bay, but revealing to them the intentions of the strange Yankee craft. *The American Turtle* went on several other missions, all with similar results.

Perhaps Bushnell did not receive the credit he deserves because *The American Turtle* did not succeed in sinking any major British ships or because of Bushnell's own secrecy. Bushnell's lack of recognition may also be because Robert Fulton later laid claim to the invention and had to be publicly denounced by Thomas Jefferson. Fulton did, however, succeed in taking credit for the invention of the steamboat, which was developed by John Fitch of South Windsor, CT, and by Samuel Morey of Orford, NH. ✦

in the country. The shaded, winding streets, which stretch inland and north along the steep riverbank, are lined with quaintly decorated and meticulously kept houses. The many antique shops and boutiques provide ample opportunity for shopping and there is also a deli and sweet shop to sate your appetite.

The nearest access in East Haddam is an unimproved ramp immediately upstream from the Goodspeed Airport seaplane dock. Though this ramp is unimproved, it is possible to launch canoes or car-topped boats and begin downriver. Larger, trailered boats should use the state ramp north of the Salmon River, just upstream. At approximately mile 14.5, you will come upon **Rich** and **Lord Islands** and the entrance to **Chapmans Pond.** Owned by the Nature Conservancy, the islands are generally conventional as islands go, though Rich Island does have the remnants of a sunken cruiser on its eastern shore. Chapmans Pond, to the immediate east, is an alluring hideaway of wide open spaces pulsing with marsh hawks, osprey, and heron, and is a great place for bass fishing. There are yellow and purple iris in June, red cardinal flowers in July and August, and lots of poison ivy. It is also an ecologically unique enclave since it is fresh water, but tidal. At the south end of the pond is a small creek that you can take back out into the River.

The **Middletown Yacht Club** is on the western bank of the River directly across from the south end of Lord Island. Further downstream lies the Chester town landing which can be reached via Parkers Point Road in Chester. The landing is well-equipped with a concrete ramp and plenty of parking. Another mile south brings you to **Gillette Castle State Park** (203) 526-2336. The Castle, which looms high above the water on the eastern shore, was built by renowned actor William Gillette in 1919 and makes a fascinating sidetrip (see page 211). As you approach the Castle from the north, you will find the ruins of Gillette's toy railway trestle stretching between two masses of rock just above the water. For those traveling on the River, landing and overnight camping is available on the beach immediately north of the Chester/Hadlyme Ferry.

The **Chester/Hadlyme Ferry** at mile 12.5 has been in continuous operation since 1768. The Ferry has no fixed schedule, but can be called by pushing a button at the end of the ramp. At $1.00 per car, plus $.50 per extra passenger, you really can't go wrong and the view of Gillette Castle is spectacular. One hundred yards south of the Ferry is the 45' flashing red light "A" at the entrance to **Whalebone Creek.** Lined with towering evergreens, Whalebone Creek is a quiet inlet great for fishing, birding, or simply getting away from it all.

At mile 11.5 are **Chester Creek** to the west and **Selden Creek** directly across to the east. Chester Creek has two marinas, a restaurant and the Pattaconk Yacht Club at its mouth and can be canoed almost all the way to the center of town. Like its neighbors, Chester is a pleasant village with fine shops and restaurants, and is home to the National Theater of the Deaf and the Norma Terris Theater. To the east, amid submerged logs, fallen trees, purple irises, ducks, marsh hawks, robins, and an occasional swan, Selden Creek glides gently behind **Selden Island State Park** (203) 526-2336. The Island, which happens to be the largest in Connecticut, is outfitted with overnight camping sites, picnic facilities, marked trails, and even a freshwater spring. If you are interesteed in a bit of exploring and hiking, Selden Island is highly recommended.

Due west of the state park is **Eustasia Island,** which can be passed to either side by medium-draft boats. Behind the island is **Deep River Landing** or **Steamboat Landing.** The public access area is also where the Valley Railroad Company's (203) 767-0103 steam train meets up with a cruise boat for regularly scheduled trips on the River. **Pratt Creek** and Deep River Marina lie directly south at mile 11.0. Pratt Creek is a pleasant tributary with ducks, swan, osprey, and herons inhabiting the surrounding marsh. Bass fishing is especially good near the River Road Bridge crossing the creek about 1/4 of a mile inland.

Following the Connecticut as it bends westward you will notice the Mt. Saint John's School high atop the shore in Deep River, which provides special care for troubled boys.

Hamburg Cove, directly to the east of **Brockway Island** at mile 7.5, is an extremely popular mooring in the summer. Though populated by sprawling estates, the surrounding bluffs give the boater a sense of solitude and have the practical advantage of shielding the Cove from excessive winds. Moving inland past the marinas and the **Joshuatown Road Bridge,** you'll come to the **Eight Mile River,** which is a great paddle for canoeists who enjoy splashing around fallen trees.

At mile 6.5 on the eastern bank is the Lyme Town Landing off Ely Road in Lyme. Note that parking here is somewhat limited and the ramp itself is unpaved. For those with larger boats, it may be best to put-in at Essex or Old Lyme . Across from the Lyme town landing is **Great Meadow** and **North Cove** of Essex. A vibrant marshy region, many migratory birds stop in this wide-open area before moving onward.

The village of Essex, perched on a peninsula between three coves, is an attractive and historic town with beautiful houses, interesting shops, and excellent restaurants. There is a ramp and town dock at the foot of the Main Street, and everything you could ever want is available from one of the town chandleries. Essex is also home to the **Connecticut River Museum** (203) 767-8269, which is located next to the Main Street ramp. The Museum is chockfull of exhibits and information about the history and geology of the River.

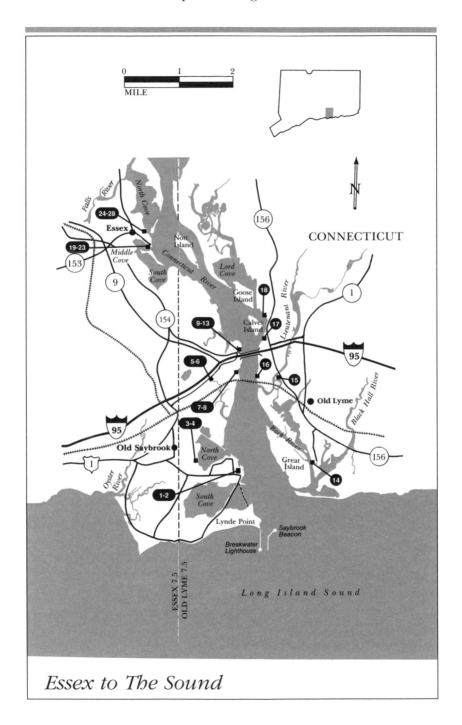

Essex to The Sound

Essex to The Sound

MILE FROM MOUTH:	6.0-0.0 (6 mile span).
NAVIGABLE BY:	All craft with drafts less than 15'. and mast heights less than 81'.
PORTAGES:	None.
CAMPING:	No established sites.
DIFFICULTY:	Flat water. (Beware of tides, winds and boat wakes.)
USGS MAPS:	Essex 7.5. Old Lyme 7.5.
NOAA CHARTS:	Connecticut River:: Long Island Sound to Deep River (#12375).
RECOMMENDED:	Tidal Currents Tables; Atlantic Coast of North America (Dept. of Commerce), Eldridge Tide and Coastal Pilot..
EMERGENCY HELP:	911. VHF channel 16. CB channel 9.

From Essex to Long Island Sound the Connecticut River exudes an air of busy diversity. With water broad and swift, the estuary region is flecked with marinas, bridges, islands, lighthouses, coves, quiet inlets, and is home to large and small boats alike. If you are using a small dinghy or canoe, be wary of wide open water. Not only will you find these areas heavily traveled by larger boats (and their wakes), but the River can easily turn rough and choppy. If you are caught near the center channel when the wind comes up, trouble may not be far behind. However, with proper precautions this final stretch of the Connecticut has much to offer.

The town of Essex stands today as the quintessential waterfront New England Village. Quaint, idyllic, and a shipbuilding center for over 300 years, Essex is well-equipped with marinas, boat yards, chandleries, yacht clubs, novelty shops, restaurants, and a host of other attractions that can

Boating Facilities and Services

	Parking ●	Permit Required ☆	Car-Topped Boat Access	Ramp: Improved/Unimproved	Picnic Area/Water/Rest Rooms/Telephone	Gas/Diesel Fuel	Supplies/Food/Bait/Ice	Rent: Fishing Boats/Canoes/Kayaks	Repairs: Engines/Hulls/Propellers	MasterCard/VISA/American Express
1 Harbor One Marina Saybrook Point (203) 388-928					WR T	G D	S I		E P	MV A
2 Saybrook Point Inn & Marina Saybrook Point (203) 388-0212					WR T	G D	SF BI		E P	MV A
3 Old Saybrook Town Ramp Sheffield Street (203) 388-2460	●		●	I						
4 North Cove Yacht Club Sheffield Street (203) 388-9087					PRIVATE CLUB					
5 Ragged Rock Marina Ferry Road (203) 388-1049					WR T	G D	S I			M V
6 Connecticut Marine Center Boston Post Road (203) 388-9300					OUTBOARD SALES / SERVICE					
7 Saybrook Marine Service Clark Street (203) 388-3614					WR T		S I		E H	
8 River Landing Marina Ferry Road (203) 388-1431					WR T	G D	SG I		EH P	MV A
9 Oak Leaf Marina Ferry Road (203) 388-9817					WR T	G D	S I		EH P	MV A
10 Ferry Point Marina Essex Road (203) 388-3260					WR T	G D	S		EH P	
11 Offshore East Fourth Avenue (203) 388-4532							S I		EH P	
12 Island Cove Marina Sunrise Avenue (203) 388-1275					W R		S I		E P	M V
13 Baldwin Bridge State Ramp Ferry Road	●		●	I						
14 Smith Neck Road State Ramp Smith Neck Road	●		●	I						

Information in these listings is provided by the facilities themselves. An asterisk (*) indicates that the facility did not respond to our most recent requests for information.

Boating Facilities and Services

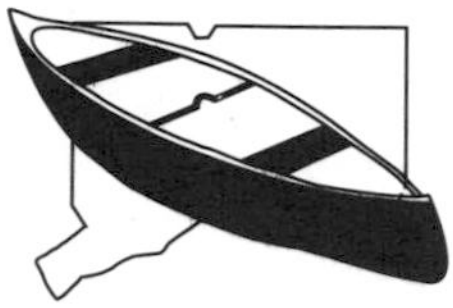

Column key (diagonal headers, left to right):
- Parking ● / Permit Required ☆
- Car-Topped Boat Access
- Ramp: Improved/Unimproved
- Picnic Area/Water/Rest Rooms/Telephone
- Gas/Diesel Fuel
- Supplies/Food/Bait/Ice
- Rent: Fishing Boats/Canoes/Kayaks
- Repairs: Engines/Hulls/Propellers
- MasterCard/VISA/American Express

#	Facility	Phone	Parking / Permit	Car-Topped	Ramp	Picnic/Water/Rest Rooms/Tel.	Gas/Diesel	Supplies/Food/Bait/Ice	Rent	Repairs	MC/V/AE
15	Old Lyme Town Landing — Rte. 156 at Lieutenant River		●	●	I						
16	Old Lyme Dock Co. — Ferry Road	(203) 434-2267				W R	G D	S I		P	MV A
17	Old Lyme Marina — Rte. 156	(203) 434-1272				WR T		S I		EH P	
18	Pilgrims Landing (Old Lyme) — Rte. 156		●	●	U						
19	Essex Yacht Club — Novelty Lane	(203) 767-8121	PRIVATE CLUB								
20	Essex Corinthian Yacht Club — Novelty Lane	(203) 767-3239	PRIVATE CLUB								
21	Brewer's Chandlery East — Novelty Lane	(203) 767-8267				W T	G D	S I			MV A
22	Essex Town Landing — Main Street		●	●	I						
23	Middle Cove Marina — Middle Cove	(203) 767-2641				WR T					
24	Essex Boat Works — Ferry Street	(203) 767-8276								EH P	M V
25	Essex Boat House — Dauntless Shipyard	(203) 767-1781							S		MV A
26	Embassy Marine Publishing — Dauntless Shipyard	(203) 767-1343	PUBLISHER OF EMBASSY BOATING GUIDES								MV A
27	Brewer's Dauntless Shipyard — Pratt Street	(203) 767-2483				W T			I	EH P	M V
28	Essex Island Marina — Essex Island	(203) 767-1267				WR T	G D	SF I		EH P	MV A

Information in these listings is provided by the facilities themselves. An asterisk (*) indicates that the facility did not respond to our most recent requests for information.

provide the boater with necessary supplies or a pleasant afternoon of sightseeing. Of historical note, the first American warship, the *Oliver Cromwell*, was built here in 1775. Also, during the War of 1812, British marines raided Essex, destroying some 23 ships at anchor or under construction. No lives were lost during the 12-hour raid, but the British did commandeer many supplies and all the town's rum.

The town of Essex maintains a ramp and dock at the foot of **Main Street.** Car-topped and trailered boats can be put in here, but there is not an abundance of parking, especially on weekends. Immediately upstream of the ramp, in a refurbished warehouse once used to service steamboats, stands the Connecticut River Museum (203) 767-8269. Along with a panoramic view of the River, the Museum offers a number of colorful and intriguing exhibits on the geology of the Connecticut River Valley, native Americans, shipbuilding, brownstone quarries, and boasts of a full-sized replica of *The American Turtle* – the first American submarine, built in 1774. If you're interested in a picnic, the **Essex town park** is just a short walk up Main Street and comes fully equipped with picnic tables, a wonderful view of Middle Cove and a gazebo to boot. Essex is also home to the Valley Railroad Company (203) 767-0103, which offers an enjoyable old-time railroad/steamboat trip from Essex to Deep River, exploring the scenic and historic shores of the River.

The numerous coves that surround Essex provide interesting boating, but mostly for canoes and dinghies. Larger boats can anchor in **Middle Cove** or go a short way into **North Cove**, but a current navigational map is essential if you wish to explore the outlying nooks and crannies. Middle Cove makes a quiet and well-protected anchorage with good holding ground and also is perfect for an end-of-the-day leisurely jaunt in a canoe or dinghy. North Cove is equally accessible by small boat and offers much in the way of coastal scenery and wildlife. The surrounding marsh is full of ducks, ospreys, hawks, swan, white perch, striped bass, as well as an impressive array of stately houses, and even a privately owned windmill perched atop the western shore. In the northwest corner of North Cove lies the mouth of Falls River, which slowly winds inland for about a mile, inviting exploration. **South Cove** is also great for canoeing. Typically uncongested and a good birding spot, South Cove has the added feature of bordering the 93-acre **Turtle Creek Wildlife Sanctuary,** which boasts of its own tidal creek and well-developed trails. The Sanctuary can be reached by Watrous Point Road just off Route 154.

Another good gunkhole for larger boats, where you can anchor away from the crowds, is on the far side of **Nott Island,** across the River from Essex. Note, however, that the anchorage here can only be approached from the south, due to shallow water on the north side of the island. For

LYME DISEASE

Lyme disease, discovered in Lyme, CT in 1976 (hence the name), is an infection resulting from the bite of certain species of tick. It can start out as a skin rash and, if left untreated, can possibly develop into arthritis. The various stages and symptoms of the disease are increasingly easy to recognize. If detected early, Lyme disease can be treated with antibiotics, and can be prevented by taking several common-sense precautions.

The ticks are principally found along the coastal areas from Delaware to Massachusetts, and are most active from May to September. Typically, the tick lives in grassy and wooded areas and feeds on the blood of small and large animals such as mice, shrews, birds, raccoons, dogs, deer, horses, and occasionally humans.

The tick bite is not painful – in fact, the tick is so small that its presence often goes unnoticed. In most cases the tick simply bites, draws blood for its nourishment, and drops off. If the tick happens to be infected with Lyme Disease, it may transmit it during the feeding process. However, a tick bite does not always result in Lyme disease. If a tick does bite you, the best way to remove it is with a small tweezers. Do not squeeze the tick's body. Grasp it gently where its mouthparts enter the skin and tug gently, but firmly. Remember to wipe the bite area thoroughly with antiseptic.

The typical early symptom of the disease is a slowly expanding red rash. Although only about 75 percent of infected individuals will develop an observable rash, other symptoms of early Lyme disease may include fatigue, mild headache, pain and stiffness in muscles and joints, slight fever, or swollen glands. Anyone who has had a tick bite followed by rash or these symptoms should consult a physician – treatment at this stage is very effective. If left untreated, the rash will most likely expand for several weeks, then slowly fade. The rash may have reddened edges and appear ring-like with a firm spot in its middle. The firmness will subside while the rash is vanishing; sometimes nothing more happens. Later symptoms of the untreated disease can include complications of the heart, nervous system, or joints. Most patients, particularly if treated by their doctor for the skin rash, do not develop these symptoms.

Four simple prevention steps

1) Avoid, when possible, tick habitat, e.g., tall grass, bushes, or woods.

2) When in tick habitat wear proper clothing, e.g., a hat, tucked in shirt with snug collar and cuffs, long pants tucked into socks, and good shoes. The use of tick repellent may help.

3) Monitor yourself and your children immediately after coming inside. Inspect your clothes, undress, and check for any ticks. Remove ticks with a tweezers. If you suspect a bite, save the tick in a jar labeled with the date and the bite's location. Watch the bite for signs of a rash for the next month or so.

4) Check your pets carefully. Tick collars may help keep ticks off.

If you've had a bite and are developing a growing rash, see your doctor. Lyme disease is treatable. For more information about Lyme disease call the Connecticut Department of Health Services (203) 566-5058. ✦

Thanks to Pfizer Central Research of Groton, Connecticut, for help in compiling this information.

smaller boats, which needn't worry about shallow water, there is a beach on the northwest corner of Nott Island perfect for landing. Since the Island is owned by the state of Connecticut, the public is free to walk around and explore, but camping is not allowed. Like many of the islands and inlets along the Connecticut, Nott Island is an excellent birding area due to the extensive array of surrounding marshes.

About 2 miles south-southeast of Essex you'll find **Goose Island** and **Lord Cove** [4.0]. Again, dinghies and canoes can travel freely in this area, but larger boats should keep an eye on the charts and venture no farther into the cove than the northeast corner of Goose Island. Small boaters will enjoy Lord Cove since it stretches north into **Lord** and **Deep Creeks,** both of which are navigable by canoe or dinghy. Just south of Goose Island is **Calves Island** [3.5], which should be added to the list of quiet anchor spots. Placid and tranquil, the Calves Island area is an excellent place to spend some time with field glasses, enjoying the flora and fauna. Unfortunately, neither Goose nor Calves Island is public land so trespassing is prohibited. To the east of Calves Island you'll find **Pilgrims Landing** with an unimproved ramp and parking, but access is limited to town residents only.

One half mile downstream from Calves Island is the **Raymond F. Baldwin Bridge,** Rte. I-95 [3.0], which has a vertical clearance of 81 feet and a public access ramp underneath on the Old Saybrook side. A new bridge replacing the Baldwin is under construction right next door, so parking underneath may be tight. Just downstream is the **Amtrak**

Railroad Bridge [2.0], also known as the **Old Lyme Draw.** During the summer, the bridge is usually in the "up" position since there is more river traffic than train traffic. When the bridge is in the "down" position, there is 19 feet of vertical clearance under the central span. The bridge operator blows a single warning blast from the horn when the bridge is to be raised or lowered. You can contact the bridge tender on VHF 13 or (203) 444-4902, or blow one long and one short blast on your horn. During the summer and especially on weekends, smaller boats without clearance problems are encouraged to avoid the drawbridge span (main channel) since this area is usually congested. The Amtrak Bridge is also used by the state of Connecticut as a marker regarding fishing licenses: south of the bridge is considered marine (i.e. saltwater), so no license is needed; north of the bridge a fresh water license is required.

The **Lieutenant River** enters from the east, immediately downriver from the Amtrak bridge. Canoes and small outboards can go 1-1/2 miles up this tributary to the town of Old Lyme, and another 1-1/2 miles to a lake-like area where the stream widens dramatically. On your way upstream you'll find a public access ramp where the Lieutenant River intersects Route 156. Keep in mind that you can also use the entrance to the Lieutenant as a means to enter the large cove north of **Great Island.** These marshes and tidal creeks support a vast assembly of plant life and a healthy population of osprey and other fishing birds. If you're interested

© Connecticut River Foundation

The steamship, Middletown, *preparing to dock in Essex, CT. The building to the left is presently the Connecticut River Museum.*

ALBERT EINSTEIN

One of the many vacationers to visit Lyme and the lower Connecticut River during the summer of 1935 was Albert Einstein. Having sailed on a small inland lake near Berlin, he decided to rent a Cape Cod Knockabout to sail on the River. Unfamiliar with the intricate currents, sandbars, and tides, he was said to have spent more time aground than afloat. *The New London Day* wrote about his misadventures under the headline, "Einstein's Miscalculation Leaves Him Stuck on Bar of Lower Connecticut River."   ✦

in fresh water fishing, the Lieutenant, due to its proximity to Long Island Sound, isn't very good. You'd be better off by heading to Lord Cove, Essex's North Cove, Turtle Creek, or any of the other tributaries and inlets north of the Baldwin Bridge.

On the east side of the Connecticut's mouth, the town of **Old Lyme** is one of the more enchanting of the riverside towns. Over the years, Old Lyme has been home to many artists, including a significant number of American Impressionists during the turn of the century. Not surprisingly, the Florence Griswold Museum (203) 434-5542 has an outstanding collection of American Impressionist works, including those of Charles Hassam, William Chadwick, and Will Howfoote.

There are two public landings south of Old Lyme that can be reached via **Smith Neck Road.** The first is accessed by an unmarked, unpaved road diverging off the main path, and allows little parking. The second, at the end of Smith Neck Road, has parking aplenty and is the better choice. Both these landings provide access to the **Back River** and **Great Island** area, where there is sufficient water depth for runabouts, but pay close attention to the tides.

Across from Old Lyme lies **Old Saybrook** and its **North** and **South Coves.** The settlement of "Saybrooke" was first conceived by 15 English lords of Puritan descent, who, having been given the land by the Earl of Warwick, were determined to establish a colony for men of "distinction and qualitie." Two of the gentlemen, Viscount Say and Lord Brooke, lent their names to the settlement though neither ever visited the colony.

The channel into Old Saybrook's **North Cove** is about 100 feet wide and 4 1/2 feet deep. A rectangular basin has been dredged out of the shallow cove, so don't go too close to the edges. It is a well-protected spot offering fair holding ground. Both the town and the North Cove Yacht Club maintain guest moorings at the head of the cove where short-term anchorage is available on a first-come, first-served basis. The town of Old Saybrook also maintains a public dock at the western end of the cove off

Sheffield Street. Directly downstream of North Cove lies **South Cove,** which has a submerged railroad causeway across its mouth and a new road causeway across its middle. With luck and persistence, you may catch some fish here, but don't go in with anything larger than a canoe or dinghy.

Between North and South Coves is Saybrook Point, where Fort Saybrook was established in 1635 under the command of Lion Gardiner, a statue of whom is nearby in Saybrook Fort Monument Park. Fort Saybrook was the first English fort in the colony of Connecticut and was destroyed by fire in 1647. Also, a few hundred meters up the road lies a stone tablet marking the original site of Yale College, which was located in Saybrook from 1707 to 1716 before moving to New Haven.

Finally, if you continue your trek south, you'll come to the mouth of the 410-mile "Quinnehtqut" River at the **Saybrook Lighthouse** on **Lynde Point.** It is here that the Dutch sailor Adriaen Block began his famous journey up the "long tidal river" to Enfield in his 44-foot *Onrust* in 1614. The 71-foot Saybrook Lighthouse was originally a wooden structure when built in 1803. Whale oil fueled the lighthouse at first, but later a 500-watt bulb was installed, visible up to 13 miles away.

The River's mouth is comparatively shallow. In fact, the constantly shifting shoals and sandbars hindered colonial navigation and prevented establishment of a deep-water port. Even today the Connecticut River is one of the few American rivers of its size without a major city at its mouth. Thanks to the sandbars, the River's estuary has remained relatively unspoiled and free of industrial development. The mouth of the River is a nursery for smaller bait fish, which in turn attracts the larger game fish. Consequently, you'll find winter flounder, striped bass, porgy, fluke, bluefish, and, of course, many fisherfolk.

Boaters should watch the tides and exercise caution when navigating the shallows on the eastern side of the River's mouth off Griswold Point. The main channel exits through two stone breakwaters on the western side beyond Saybrook Point Lighthouse. A word of caution: Long Island Sound is no place for canoes or dinghies. If you're going to enter these waters, do so with an appropriately sized boat.

State Agencies

Connecticut
Department of Environmental
Protection
165 Capital Avenue
Hartford, CT 06106
(203) 566-5599

Motor Vehicle Department
Motor Vehicle Building
Wethersfield, CT 06109
(203) 566-3781

Massachusetts
Division of Fisheries and Wildlife
Field Headquarters
Westboro, MA 01581
(508) 366-4479

Division of Motor Boats
100 Nashua Street
Boston, MA 02114
(617) 727-2121

New Hampshire
Department of Fish and Game
2 Haven Drive
Concord, NH 03301
(603) 271-3421

Department of Resources and
Economic Development
Park and Recreation Division
P.O. Box 856
Concord, NH 03301
(603) 271-3556

Department of Safety
Division of Safety Services
Concord, NH 03301
(603) 271-3336

Vermont
Office of Tourism
Montpelier, VT 05602
(802) 828-3236

Department of Motor Vehicles
Registration Unit
120 State Street
Montpelier, VT 05603
(802) 828-2000

Department of Fish and Wildlife
Agency of Environmental
Conservation
Barre, VT 05641
(802) 479-3241

Department of Public Safety
Marine Division
Barre, VT 05676
(802) 828-2000

Bibliography

AMC River Guide: Central/Southern New England – Volume 2. Boston, MA: The Appalachian Mountain Club, 1978.

Bachman, Ben, *Upstream: A Voyage Up the Connecticut River.* Boston, MA: Houghton Mifflin Co., 1985.

Canoeing on the Connecticut River. Montpelier, VT: Vermont State Board of Recreation and Water Resources Department, 1964.

Delaney, Edmund T., *The Connecticut River: New England's Historic Waterway.* Chester, CT: Globe Pequot Press, 1983.

Grant, Marion Hepburn, *The Infernal Machines of Saybrook's David Bushnell.* Old Saybrook, CT: The Bicentennial Committee of Old Saybrook, Connecticut, 1976.

Jacobus, Melanethon W., *The Connecticut Steamboat Story.* Hartford, CT: The Connecticut Historical Society, 1956.

Schweiker, Roioli, *Canoe Camping Vermont and New Hampshire Rivers.* Somersworth, NH: New Hampshire Publishing Company, 1977.

Wikoff, Jerold, *The Upper Valley: An Illustrated Tour Along the Connecticut River Before the Twenieth Century.* Chelsea,VT: Chelsea Green Publishing, 1985.

Index

Index to Advertisers

CONNECTICUT RIVER WATERSHED COUNCIL, Inc.
125 Combs Road • Easthampton • MA 01027

I want to help improve and protect the water resources of the Connecticut River Valley through membership with the CRWC.

NAME _____

ADDRESS _____

_____

PHONE _____

Family/Individual Categories:

Student	$15 ☐
Individual	$25 ☐
Family and Non-Profit	$35 ☐
Contributor	$50 ☐
Donor	$100 ☐
Sustaining	$300 ☐
Sponsor	$500 ☐
Benefactor	$1,000 ☐

Corporate Categories:

Affiliate	$50-99 ☐
Donor	$100-249 ☐
Sponsor	$250-499 ☐
Steward	$500-999 ☐
Benefactor	$1,000-2,499 ☐
Round Table	$2,500 & over ☐

Make checks payable to the
Connecticut River Watershed Council, Inc.
 Easthampton, MA 01027

Contributions are tax deductible to the extent of the law.

YES!

I would like to order
The Complete Boating Guide to the Connecticut River.

NAME_____

STREET_____

CITY_____

STATE_____ ZIP_____

	Number of Copies	Price	Total
		$11.95	
MA residents Sales Tax 5% or CT residents Sales Tax 8%			
Postage & Handling $1.60 per book			
TOTAL ENCLOSED			